FaithWeaver™ Children's Messages 1

Group
Loveland, Colorado

FaithWeaver™ Children's Messages 1

Copyright © 1999 Group Publishing, Inc.

Credits

Contributing Authors: Jacqui Baker, Tim Baker, Karen Dockrey, Jan Kershner, Kelly Martin, Julie Meiklejohn, Siv M. Ricketts, and Helen Turnbull

Editor: Debbie Gowensmith
Quality Control Editor: Dave Thornton
Chief Creative Officer: Joani Schultz
Copy Editor: Betty Taylor
Art Director and Designer: Lewis Agrell
Cover Art Director: Jeff A. Storm
Cover Designer: Lisa Chandler
Computer Graphic Artist: Joyce Douglas
Cover Photographer: Bohm/Marrazzo, L.D. Bohm Studios
Illustrator: Jan Knudson
Production Manager: Peggy Naylor

Unless otherwise noted, Scripture taken from the HOLY BIBLE, NEW INTERNATIONAL VERSION®. Copyright © 1973, 1978, 1984 by International Bible Society. Used by permission of Zondervan Publishing House. All rights reserved.

Library of Congress Cataloging-in-Publication Data
FaithWeaver children's messages / Group Publishing.
     p.   cm.
   ISBN 0-7644-2080-1 (alk. paper)
    1. Children's sermons. 2. Bible--Children's sermons. 3. Sermons,
American. I. Group Publishing.
  BV4315.F24 1999
  252' .53--dc21
                                                 99-24203
                                               CIP

10 9 8 7 6 5 4 3 2 1   08 07 06 05 04 03 02 01 00 99
Printed in the United States of America.

Contents

Introduction

Children of all ages love to hear great stories again and again. They're fascinated with the characters and the action, and they want to capture the stories in their minds and hearts. The best stories in the world—with real-life heroes, dramatic action, and great truths—are in the Bible. Children's messages provide a great opportunity for children to capture biblical stories and truths in their hearts.

FaithWeaver™ Children's Messages 1 will help children do just that. These sermons will help you involve children in worship and help them apply biblical truths to their lives. Each sermon explores one Bible story, allowing children to experience what happened to the people in the story. These experiences lead children to understand a Bible verse containing a core truth from the Bible story. For example, children will eat pretzels and act thirsty, pretend to walk and crawl in the desert, and then knock on a door to ask for water to learn that God answers when we knock (Luke 11:9) just as he answered Hagar and Ishmael's cries in the desert (Genesis 21:8-21). This kind of active learning will help children understand the Bible stories and apply the truths to their lives.

All your children will look forward to experiencing these sermons. The stories, activities, and truths will involve children from preschool age through elementary school age. Be sure to attend to the special needs of younger students during your children's sermon time, and encourage older students to help younger ones with the activities. You can also involve your congregation members, who will be refreshed by new perspectives from these messages—and from the children! You may use a microphone or repeat what children say, hold up props so congregation members can experience the story as the kids do, or even encourage your congregation to cheer or sing along with the kids. These Bible-based children's sermons will touch both children's and adults' lives.

We've arranged *FaithWeaver Children's Messages 1* to parallel the four quarters (fall, winter, spring, and summer) most churches use for Sunday school and other educational programs. The book contains four sections of thirteen sermons—one sermon a week for an entire year. The fall quarter begins with God's creation of the world and explores the book of Genesis. During the winter and spring quarters, we move to the New Testament stories of Jesus' birth, life, death, and resurrection so children can focus on Christ during

Christmas and Easter. The spring quarter returns to the exciting stories in Genesis and continues through the Israelites' freedom from Egypt.

You may use the messages in the order suggested, rearrange them to coincide with holidays or events, or choose stories and verses that fit your message's theme. The Bible stories listed in the table of contents and the Scripture index will help you choose the Bible stories and Scriptures you want to teach.

You may also use this book in conjunction with Group's FaithWeaver™Bible Curriculum for fall 1999 through summer 2000, which you can order from your local Christian bookstore. Using *FaithWeaver Children's Messages 1* along with this family ministry curriculum helps you reinforce Bible stories and verses in a way that cements Bible truths in kids' lives.

Because children of all ages love good stories, *FaithWeaver Children's Messages 1* will capture the attention of both children and adults, involve everyone in the action, and most importantly, teach participants the rich biblical truths these stories impart. Have fun with these messages, and children will hold the stories in their hearts forever.

SECTION

ONE

FALL
QUARTER

God Creates the World

Bible Story: Genesis 1:1-2:3

> **Bible Verse:** "In the beginning God created the heavens and the earth" (Genesis 1:1).

Simple Supplies: *You'll need a Bible, one yellow pipe cleaner and four orange pipe cleaners for each child, and an adult volunteer to turn the lights off and on.*

Close your eyes. Let's try to imagine what it was like before God made the world. The world was empty and dark. No people, animals, or flowers were alive yet. But God was alive, and he decided to create the world. *Pause for a moment to allow kids to imagine this, and then tell children to open their eyes. Open your Bible to Genesis 1:1, and show the page to the children.*

Genesis 1:1 says, **"In the beginning God created the heavens and the earth."** God made everything.

On the first day, God made the light. In a moment, the lights will go out. When they do, think about what it would have been like to be with God before he made the world. Then I'll read the Bible verse again and say, "And God said..." Then I'd like you to call out, "Let there be light!" Let's practice once with the lights on.

"In the beginning God created the heavens and the earth." And God said... *Help children respond by calling out, "Let there be light." Now we'll try it with the lights off. Have your volunteer turn off the lights.*

"In the beginning God created the heavens and the earth." And God said... *Help children respond by calling out, "Let there be light." Then have the volunteer turn on the lights again.* When God said, "Let there be light," there was light!

On the second day, God made the sky. Can you point to the sky? *Pause for children to respond.* Great! Then on the third day, God made dry land. Can you point to the land? *Pause.* Great again! God also made plants on the third day. What kinds of plants grow on the land? *Pause.* You're right. Flowers and vegetables and trees all grow on the land God made.

On the fourth day, God created big lights in the sky to mark off days, nights, years, and seasons. Can you tell me what some of those big lights are called? *Pause.* Yes, the sun, moon, and stars. Now we're going to make our very own suns with pipe cleaners. *Distribute one yellow pipe cleaner and four orange pipe cleaners to each child.* First make a circle with the yellow pipe cleaner, and twist the ends together so they'll stay. *Demonstrate this, and be sure to help younger children with the task.* Next take one orange pipe cleaner, put it through the circle, and twist it around the yellow one. Now spread the two orange ends apart so they look like sun rays. Do this with the other three orange pipe cleaners. *Demonstrate this, and again be sure to help younger children.* Now show me what big light God made on the fourth day. *Encourage children to hold up their suns.* Great!

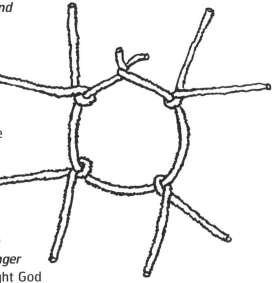

On the fifth day, God made sea creatures and birds. Can anyone tell me what kinds of sea creatures God made? *Pause.* And can anyone tell me what sounds birds make? *Pause.* That's wonderful! On the sixth day, God created all the land animals. Call out the names of some of the animals God made. *Pause.* That's right!

Also on the sixth day, God added another thing to all he'd made. Can you point to what special thing God created last of all? *Pause.* You've got it! On the sixth day, God made people.

Do you know what God thought about everything he'd made? When God was finished creating the world, he said everything he'd made was very good. Let's thank God for making so many good things.

When I point to you, call out one thing God made—butterflies or trees, for example. Then everyone else will say—just as God did—"Very good!" *Invite your congregation to participate along with the kids in this responsive prayer. If you have a small group, allow each child to say one thing. You might consider pointing to a few adults, too. If your group is larger, point to at least five children.*

God Creates Adam and Eve

Bible Story: Genesis 2:4-22

> **Bible Verse:** "I praise you because I am fearfully and wonderfully made; your works are wonderful, I know that full well" (Psalm 139:14).

Simple Supplies: *You'll need a Bible, clay or modeling dough, and plastic for covering the floor. Before the sermon, place the plastic on the floor for children to sit on.*

ass out a small bit of clay to each child. With your bit of clay, take a moment to make an animal. For example, you could roll the clay thin and make a snake, or roll it into balls and make a bear—any animal you want. *Allow kids a couple of minutes to create, and then ask for volunteers to share what they've made. Compliment children's efforts.*

Did you know that God once played with clay, too? He made the first man from the dust of the ground! And when God breathed into the man, he came to life.

Tell me, where's the most beautiful place you've ever been? *Ask for volunteers to share.* Those places sound really great. God put the man he'd made in a very beautiful place, a garden with lots of trees and four rivers. God wanted man to take care of the garden.

Then God brought all the animals to the man so he could name them. What were some animals the man named? *Pause for children to respond.* You're right. The man sure had a lot of funny pets! Do you have pets? Would the animal you made from your clay be a very good friend? *Pause.* Animals can be very special friends, but the man was lonely for someone like him. So God made a woman to be the man's real best friend.

Now hold up your hand so you can see your palm. With the pointer finger of your other hand, trace as many of the lines on your palm as you can see, including all the little tiny lines. *Give children a minute or so to follow instructions. You might invite the congregation to join in, too.* There are a lot of lines on my hand, I think more than I could count if I tried. When God made the man and woman, he didn't leave out any detail, or tiny part. He made all the lines on their hands and all the hairs on their heads, and he made every part of you, too. *Open your Bible to Psalm 139:14, and show the page to the children.*

Psalm 139:14 says, **"I praise you because I am fearfully and won-derfully made; your works are wonderful, I know that full well."** We thank God because he made us, even down to the tiniest details. Why don't you hold your palms up to God while we thank him for making us.

Dear God, we thank you for making us so wonderfully. Thank you for knowing how many lines are on our hands and for paying so much at-tention to the little details of who we are. Thank you for planning the days of our lives, and thank you especially for loving us. Amen.

Just as God made the first man and woman exactly the way he wanted them to be, he made you wonderfully, too! He gave you just the right hair color, the perfect nose, the exact number of freckles on your skin, and all the lines on your palms. Each time you wash your hands this week, try to remember how special you are to God.

Adam and Eve Sin

Bible Story: Genesis 3:1-24

> **Bible Verse:** "For all have sinned and fall short of the glory of God" (Romans 3:23).

Simple Supplies: *You'll need a Bible, a plastic bowl that contains indi-vidually wrapped candies, a trash can or bag, and an adult volunteer to help you with this activity. In the bowl, include a few red candies, but be sure there are enough candies in colors other than red for each child to have one.*

I'm so glad you're here today! I'd like to offer you each one piece of candy. You can take almost any piece of candy you want, but please leave the red candies in the bowl.

After you say this, cue your volunteer to say the following: "Actually, kids, why shouldn't you eat any candy you want? It doesn't really mat-ter anyway. And you know what? I've heard that the red candies are much tastier than the others."

Pass around the bowl, and allow children to choose whatever candy they want. When children each have a piece of candy, ask them to wait to eat the candies. Why did you choose the piece of candy you have in your hand? *Pause for children to respond.*

You know, two people in the Bible, Adam and Eve, had to make a choice like the one you just made. But Adam and Eve weren't choosing what kind of candy to eat. They had to decide whether to obey or disobey God. Adam and Eve lived in a garden, and God told them they could eat from any tree in the garden except one. And just as [volunteer's name] told you that the red candies taste the best, a snake told Eve that the fruit she wasn't supposed to eat was really the best. So even though God had told Adam and Eve not to eat from that tree, Eve ate the fruit. She gave some to Adam, and he ate it too.

You may go ahead and eat your candy now, but I want you to do something special with your wrapper. I want you to try to hide it somewhere close to you. *Pause for children to eat the candy and hide the wrappers. Help younger children hide their candy wrappers.* When Adam and Eve disobeyed God, they tried to hide what they did just as you hid your candy wrappers. What are some ways you try to hide the wrong things you've done? *Pause.* We sometimes try to hide our sin just as Adam and Eve did. But God knew what Adam and Eve had done, and they had to face the effects of disobeying God.

In the same way, you and I can't hide our sin. We all sin, and God knows about it. *Open your Bible to Romans 3:23, and show the page to the children.*

 Romans 3:23 says, **"For all have sinned and fall short of the glory of God."** The Bible tells us that all of us have done wrong things. When we do something wrong, it makes God sad. But instead of trying to hide our sin as we hid our candy wrappers, God wants us to tell him we're sorry for what we've done wrong. And guess what: If we ask God to forgive us, he will!

Before we pray, I'd like you to find your candy wrappers and hold them in your hands. *Allow children to retrieve their wrappers.* Now I'd like you to think about something you've done to disobey God. *Help children by suggesting something you've done, or offer ideas such as disobeying parents or being mean to their siblings.* Now let's pray to tell God we're sorry and ask God to forgive us for the wrong things we've done.

 Dear God, you know what's best for us, so we should always obey you. We're sorry for disobeying you and making you sad. Please forgive us of our sin. Thank you for loving us and forgiving us when we ask you. In Jesus' name, amen.

Hold up the trash can. Now that you've asked God for forgiveness, I'd like you to toss your candy wrappers into this trash can and say, "Thank you, God, for forgiving me!" Ready? Here we go! *Count to three, and then lead kids in shouting, "Thank you, God, for forgiving me!"*

Cain Kills Abel

Bible Story: Genesis 4:1-16

> Bible Verse: "Be devoted to one another in brotherly love. Honor one another above yourselves" (Romans 12:10).

Simple Supplies: *You'll need a Bible and heart-shaped stickers in different colors.*

I'm going to tell you a story about two best friends named Hillary and Karen. Their teacher assigned a school project. Karen worked on her project for weeks and did the very best she could. Hillary worked on her project only the night before it was due. How do you think Karen's project turned out? What about Hillary's? *Pause for children to respond.* When the teacher returned their projects, Karen got the highest grade in the class. Hillary received a lower grade with a note from the teacher that said, "I know you can do better if you try."

If you were Hillary, how would you treat Karen when you found out she'd earned a better grade than you? *Pause.* Well, Hillary was so mad at Karen that she wouldn't even speak to her. Hillary told the other kids that Karen's mom did the project for her, and Hillary made fun of Karen for choosing a silly idea.

How do you think this made Karen feel? *Pause.* What might have been a better way for Hillary to act? *Pause.* Hillary could have been happy for Karen, she could have learned from Karen, and she could have asked Karen to help her do better next time.

If you've ever felt jealous of someone, as Hillary felt about Karen and her better grade, put your hand on your heart. All of us feel jealous sometimes. Keep your hand on your heart, and we'll pray for God's help when we feel that way.

Dear God, help us to always do our best. Help us to be loving and kind instead of feeling jealous when others do better than we do or when others get the things we want. In Jesus' name, amen.

The story of Hillary and Karen is a lot like the story of Cain and Abel in the Bible. Cain and Abel were brothers. Cain was a farmer, and Abel took care of sheep. Cain and Abel both took gifts to God. Like Hillary, Cain didn't do his best, and God told Cain that he could have done better. Abel took the best of his sheep to God, and God was happy with Abel's gift.

Cain was so jealous that he killed Abel! Hold out one of your hands. When we get jealous, it's as if our heart shrinks and gets so hard that we shut love and other people out. Make a fist to show what that's like. Because Cain's heart was hard like your fist, he made things worse by lying to God about what he'd done. What could Cain have done differently? *Pause.*

Cain could have loved his brother instead of hurting him. That's just what God wants us to do, even if we're feeling jealous or angry. When we love others, our hearts are soft and open. Open your fist. See, now you can hold on to things or give them away or shake someone's hand. Why don't you shake someone's hand right now? *While kids shake hands, distribute heart stickers. Ask kids to put the stickers on their clothing. Open your Bible to Romans 12:10, and show the page to the children.*

Romans 12:10 says, **"Be devoted to one another in brotherly love. Honor one another above yourselves."** What do you think it means to be devoted to someone? *Pause.*

Being devoted to someone is like sticking to them even when things go wrong. You each have a heart sticker. That sticker stands for you. Now I'm going to give you another sticker that I want you to attach to the side of your sticker so the two touch each other. That other sticker stands for the people you should be devoted to. Before I hand out these stickers, though, think of one person you need to be devoted to— maybe your mom or dad, brother or sister, friend or teacher, or someone else that you haven't stuck to as closely as you should.

Distribute stickers, and have children put them on. For the rest of the day when you see these stickers, think of how you can be devoted to the person you thought of. For example, you might feel like yelling at your sister, but instead offer to spend time with her.

Noah Builds an Ark

Bible Story: Genesis 6:5-22

> **Bible Verse:** "Peter and the other apostles replied: 'We must obey God rather than men!' " (Acts 5:29).

Simple Supplies: *You'll need a Bible.*

Choose a partner, and one of you tell the other person something you've learned today.

As children share, whisper the Bible verse: **"Peter and the other apostles replied: 'We must obey God rather than men!' "** Did you hear what I said? No? Let's try again. This time, the other partner should tell something he or she learned today.

As children share, whisper the Bible verse again: **"Peter and the other apostles replied: 'We must obey God rather than men!' "** Did you hear what I said this time? No? I wonder if this is what it was like for Noah to try to listen to God. *Open your Bible to Genesis 6, and show the page to the children.* The Bible says Noah was a very good man, but the world was full of evil, or bad things. God had a big job for Noah to do, and it must have been pretty hard for Noah to listen and obey.

Let's play a game. Pretend I'm Noah, and I have to build a huge ark, or boat, because God told me to. I know building this big ark isn't going to be much fun, and you're going to try to convince me to do something else. Something much more fun. First you all are going to yell, "Hey, Noah!" and then I'll point to one of you. If I point to you, you might say, "Let's go get some ice cream!" or "Let's go play baseball!" Ready? Let's try it.

Let kids begin by shouting, "Hey Noah!" Then choose one child to speak. Oh no. It says here in the Bible that God is really sad that the world is disobeying him, and he wants me to build a big boat.

"We must obey God rather than men!" *Have kids shout again, and choose another child to speak.* Sorry, I've got to build an ark of cypress wood, make rooms in it, and cover the whole thing with black, icky gunk called pitch so water will stay out of the ark. Can you help me? *Have*

kids pretend to hammer. Then have kids shout again, and choose an-other child to speak. Oh, I'm sorry. I can't. It says here that I have to make this ark 450 feet long, 75 feet wide, and 45 feet high! That's going to take me a while. Let's count to forty-five and think about how high the ark will be. *Lead children in counting. Then have kids shout again, and choose another child.* I wish I could join you. But I have to make a roof; a door; and not one, not two, but three decks! I'm kind of busy. *Have kids shout again, and choose another child.* Oh no, oh no!

"**We must obey God rather than men!**" God says he's going to flood the earth, so I have to get my family, all kinds of animals, and lots of food onto the ark. I sure could use your help doing that. *Have kids pretend to load the ark. Starting at one end of the group, have a child pretend to hand something to the person next to him or her. Then have that person pretend to hand something to the next person, and so on.*

Noah had a huge job to do for God, and sometimes it must have been hard for Noah to listen to and obey God. But the Bible says Noah did everything God told him to. Sometimes it's hard for us to listen to and obey God, too. But listen to what the Bible says about obeying God. *Open your Bible to Acts 5:29, and show the page to the children.*

Acts 5:29 says, "**We must obey God rather than men!**" Let's shout that out. Ready? "**We must obey God rather than men!**"

Now let's ask God to help us obey him as Noah obeyed him. Dear God, sometimes it's hard for us to obey you. Sometimes we don't want to do what you ask, and sometimes we don't think we can do what you ask. Please help us to listen to you and then be strong enough to obey you. In Jesus' name, amen.

God Floods the Earth

Bible Story: Genesis 7:1–8:22; 9:8–16

> **Bible Verse:** "The Lord is faithful to all his promises and loving toward all he has made" (Psalm 145:13b).

Simple Supplies: *You'll need a Bible and rainbow stickers.*

Who can tell me what a puddle is? What do you like to do in puddles? *Pause for children to respond.* A long time ago, it rained so much that a puddle formed. Then the puddle grew and grew and grew until it became a flood. This flood grew bigger than your driveway, bigger than your street, bigger than your house, and bigger than our town. It grew so big that it covered the whole earth. There was only one place the water didn't cover. That place was Noah's ark.

Can anyone tell me what an ark is? *Pause.* An ark is a very big boat. God told a man named Noah to build an ark and to get in the ark with his family and every kind of animal so they'd stay safe and dry during the flood. Every person and every animal in the ark had a partner. Why don't you find a partner, too, and link elbows with your partner. *Pause. If there are an uneven number of children, link elbows with a child close to you.* What kind of animal would you and your partner like to be? *Pause.*

Noah and his wife, Noah's sons and their wives, and all the pairs of animals got onto the boat. Then it started raining, and it rained for a very, very long time. The ark floated on top of the water that covered the entire world. Sway back and forth with your partner as if you're in a boat that's rocking back and forth. *Pause.* What do you think if felt like in the ark? *Pause.* There were so many animals in that boat! Scoot close to the people around you as if you're in a crowded boat, and keep rocking back and forth. *Pause.* What do you think it sounded like in the ark? *Pause.* Why don't you each make animal sounds while you keep swaying back and forth.

Noah and his family and all the animals stayed inside that big boat for more than a year! What do you think it was like for Noah and his family to be on the ark for such a very, very long time with all those animals? *Pause.* Do you think Noah and his family worried that they'd never get off that boat? *Pause.* Even if you like animals, a year is a long time to stay inside a boat with your family and a bunch of animals. Noah knew everything would be OK, though. How did he know? Because God had promised. A year was a very, very long time. But God kept his promise. God always keeps his promises.

And so after more than a year, it was finally time for everyone to get off the boat and step again onto dry land. You can now separate, stand up, and stretch your legs to feel what it might have been like to get off the ark after so long. What do you think Noah thought as he got off the boat? *Pause.* Everybody was dry and safe. God had kept his promise. *Open your Bible to Psalm 145:13b, and show the page to the children.*

Psalm 145:13b says, **"The Lord is faithful to all his promises and**

loving toward all he has made." That means God loves us and always keeps his promises! God showed his love by taking care of everyone on the ark, and he kept his promise to keep them safe.

God made another promise on the day Noah and his family and all the animals left the ark. God promised that a flood would never again cover the earth. Can you remember what God said would remind him of that promise? *Pause.* That's right! God said rainbows remind him of his promise to never again allow a flood to cover the earth. *Distribute the rainbow stickers to the children.* Rainbows can remind us that God always keeps his promises.

Let's thank God for always keeping his promises. Dear God, thank you for loving all you have made, including each one of us. Thank you for always keeping your promises. In Jesus' name, amen.

People Build a Tower at Babel

Bible Story: Genesis 11:1-9

> **Bible Verse:** "Love the Lord your God with all your heart and with all your soul and with all your strength" (Deuteronomy 6:5).

Simple Supplies: *You'll need a Bible and blocks.*

What kinds of things do people do to show how important or how great they are? *Pause for children to respond.* Some people in the Bible wanted to build a tower as high as the sky to show everyone how important they were. *Put the blocks where kids can reach them.* You're going to build a tower, too, by following my instructions. Before we begin, let's pray.

Dear God, let everything we do give you honor. We love you, God. Amen.

OK, now just do exactly what I tell you. *Begin speaking gibberish while pointing and gesturing and sounding very instructional. After a couple of minutes, stop and ask:* Why aren't we getting our tower built? Why was it hard to follow my instructions? *Pause.* Without being able to understand what people say, it's very hard to get anything done. The people in the

Bible story wanted to build a tower that reached to the heavens to "make a name" for themselves. What do you think that means? *Pause.* These people wanted others to notice and remember them for their tower. Instead of drawing attention to God, they wanted attention for themselves. What other things do people do to get noticed? *Pause.* How do you think God feels when we do these things? *Pause.* Because the people didn't want to honor God, God caused them to speak different languages. They couldn't understand one another any more, so they couldn't finish building the tower.

Instead of building a tower or a name for yourself, God wants you to build your lives around him. *Open your Bible to Deuteronomy 6:5, and show the page to the children.*

Deuteronomy 6:5 says, **"Love the Lord your God with all your heart and with all your soul and with all your strength."** Think for a minute about this question: If you love God with all your heart, soul, and strength, what kinds of things will you do? Now before you answer, pick up a block. As you hand me your block, say, "I love God, so I can..." and complete the sentence. *Have children take turns handing their blocks to you and saying the sentence.*

It's really exciting that you love God and can do things for him. Each time you see a building this week, remember that God wants you to build your life with love for him.

Abram Follows God's Direction

Bible Story: Genesis 12:1-8

> **Bible Verses:** "Trust in the Lord with all your heart and lean not on your own understanding; in all your ways acknowledge him, and he will make your paths straight" (Proverbs 3:5-6).

Simple Supplies: *You'll need a Bible and a brown paper bag filled with small wrapped candies. Before the sermon, hide the bag of candy at the front of the worship area.*

Ask children to follow you as you lead them around the worship area. *As you walk, review the Bible story.* A man named Abram lived a long time ago. One day, God talked to Abram and asked Abram to leave his country and his extended family and go to a new place. God didn't even tell Abram where he was going, but God promised that Abram would have many blessings, or really good things, if he followed God. God asked Abram to trust him. If God asked you to leave home and go to a different city, would it be easy or hard for you to do? Why? *Pause for children to respond.*

Continue leading children around the worship area. The Bible doesn't tell us whether Abram had a difficult time making his decision, but it does tell us that he trusted God and left his home. What do you think it means to trust someone? *Pause for responses.* To trust someone means to believe someone, to know that someone is telling the truth, and to be certain that someone will do as he or she says. *You should be close to the end of your "journey."*

So Abram and his family traveled for many, many miles until God told Abram that the land would belong to Abram's family. *Lead children to the front of the worship area.* After traveling for so long, how do you think Abram felt when God said Abram's family would have a home? *Pause. Hold up the brown paper bag.* I have here a brown paper bag with candy inside. *Ask kids to line up and one by one close their eyes, reach into the bag, and get a piece of candy.*

You didn't know where I was leading you, but you followed me anyway. Well Abram didn't know where God was leading him, but he followed anyway. You believed me when I said there was candy in the bag; you knew I wouldn't ask you to do something that could hurt you. And Abram believed God when God said Abram would be better off in the new place. Abram also knew that God wouldn't ask him to do something that could hurt him. You trusted me today just as Abram trusted God.

The Bible says we can always trust God. *Open your Bible to Proverbs 3:5-6, and show the page to the children.*

Proverbs 3:5-6 says, **"Trust in the Lord with all your heart and lean not on your own understanding; in all your ways acknowledge him, and he will make your paths straight."** The Bible tells us we can trust God even more than we trust ourselves; when we do, God will show us the right way to go. What do you think might have happened if Abram hadn't trusted God? *Pause.* Because Abram trusted God even more than he trusted himself, God brought Abram to a new home.

Close your eyes for a minute, and think about something you have trouble trusting God with. Maybe it's hard for you to trust God with your schoolwork or your family or your friends or what you'll be when you grow up. *Pause to allow kids to reflect.* Now we're going to pray. When I say, "God, help us to trust you with our..." call out those things you have trouble trusting God with. I'll bet many of us have trouble trusting God with the same things, so we can all pray about them together. Let's pray. Dear God, just as Abram trusted you, we want to trust you with all our hearts, even when it's hard and even when it doesn't make sense to us. God, help us to trust you with our...*Pause for children to complete the sentence.* Amen.

Lot and Abram Divide the Land

Bible Story: Genesis 13:1-18

> **Bible Verse:** "Do to others as you would have them do to you" (Luke 6:31).

Simple Supplies: *You'll need a Bible and stiff paper towels or sheets of construction paper that stand up when bent.*

How many of you have an uncle? Who can tell me something you like about your uncle? *Pause for children to respond.* In the Bible, a man named Lot had a special uncle named Abram. Abram and Lot traveled around together, along with their families and workers and animals, and looked for a good place to live. These two grown-up men and all the people who traveled with them lived in tents. Let's make tents from these paper towels. *Give each child a stiff paper towel, and show children how to fold the paper towels in half so they stand up.* When Abram and Lot and their families and their workers and their animals came to a good place to live, they put up their tents so they could live in them. Let's all put up our tents in the same area just as Abram and Lot and the people with them did. *Direct children to set up their tents in the same small area.* Wow! There are a lot of tents in this little bit of space, aren't there?

Just as our tents are crowded together in this small space, the tents of Abram and Lot and all the people with them were crowded together in a small space. The people didn't have enough room to grow food to feed their many animals. The people who took care of the animals, who were called herdsmen, started to fuss and quarrel and argue with one another about who was taking up too much space.

Let's do an experiment. Let's all scoot in very close together. *Encourage children to squeeze together.* How does it make you feel to be so close to everyone? *Pause.* When we're all crowded together like this, we might accidentally step on someone's toes or poke someone in the side. Well, this is a lot like how Abram and Lot felt. What do you think Abram and Lot should have done? *Pause.*

Those are good ideas. The Bible tells us a way to solve problems like the one Abram and Lot had. *Open your Bible to Luke 6:31, and show the page to the children, who should still be crowded together.*

 Luke 6:31 says, **"Do to others as you would have them do to you."** This means we can think about how we want to be treated and then treat other people that way. I'd like a little bit more space, wouldn't you? So let's all spread out again.

Abram was a very smart man. He thought about how he wanted to be treated, and he treated Lot just that way! He said to Lot, "We're family, so let's not fight. Let's simply spread apart. You can choose where you'd like to live, and I'll go the other way." So Lot and his people chose to take their tents one direction, and Abram and his people went the other direction. Why don't you all get your tents and set them down next to you. *Help children retrieve their tents and sit back down.* Look at all the space those tents have now! Because Abram treated others the way he liked to be treated, the people had enough space for their tents, their belongings, and their animals.

Can you think of a time you've had trouble sharing with someone? Without saying any names, tell what you had to share and why it was hard to share. *Choose a few children to share.*

Sharing is hard sometimes, but let's remember what the Bible says we should do.

 "Do to others as you would have them do to you." What can you do next time you have a hard time sharing with someone? *Pause.* Those are great ideas!

 God can help you remember to **"Do to others as you would have them do to you."** Let's pray now and ask for God's help. Dear God, please show us how to get along with others. Help us treat others the way we'd like to be treated. In Jesus' name, amen.

God Makes a Covenant With Abram

Bible Story: Genesis 15:1-18

> **Bible Verse:** " 'For I know the plans I have for you,' declares the Lord, 'plans to prosper you and not to harm you, plans to give you hope and a future' " (Jeremiah 29:11).

Simple Supplies: *You'll need a Bible.*

'm so glad you're all here, and I have a plan for what I'd like you to do today. I'd like you to build a Christmas tree. Won't that be great? Are you ready to start? *Pause for children to respond. Continue despite their confusion.* OK, you have fifteen seconds to build a Christmas tree. *Count off fifteen seconds, then applaud children's efforts.* You did a great job! But I noticed you had a hard time creating a tree. Why? *Pause.* I didn't tell you my plans for building a Christmas tree, did I? Why are plans so important? What happens when we try to do something without any plans? *Pause.* Plans let us know what we're supposed to do, don't they? Did you know that God has plans for you? *Open your Bible to Jeremiah 29:11, and show the page to the children.*

Jeremiah 29:11 says, " **'For I know the plans I have for you,' de-clares the Lord, 'plans to prosper you and not to harm you, plans to give you hope and a future.' "** God is telling us he has good plans for us, and God's plans will help us know what we're supposed to do.

The Bible tells of a man named Abram who learned that God had good plans for him. Abram was older than most of your grandparents, and he didn't have any children. I'd like you to shut your eyes, and think about a man who's older than a grandfather. God told Abram that he would have so many children, grandchildren, great-grandchildren, and so on, that he wouldn't even be able to count them all! What do you think Abram thought about God's plans for him? *Pause.* The Bible says Abram believed God even though God's plans seemed impossible. It's impor-tant for us to believe in God's plans for us, too, even though they may seem impossible or strange.

Let's practice believing in plans by trying to build that Christmas tree again. This time, I'll tell you what my plans for you are. *Arrange children*

in the following rows, with fewer children in each successive row: For the first row, have children sit on the floor. For the second row, have children kneel. For the third row, have children stand with their hands on their knees. For the fourth row, have children stand up. For the fifth row, have children stand with their hands above their heads. Have any additional children stand beside the "tree," opening and closing their hands as blinking lights. Lead the congregation in clapping for the children. Have children stay in their tree formation for the prayer.

What a wonderful tree! Now that we've learned what it's like to trust plans as Abram trusted God's plans, let's pray and thank God for his plans. *"Disassemble" the tree, starting with the smallest row and working up to the largest row. As each row of children leaves the tree, have those children call out, "Thank you, God, for your good plans!"*

Abraham Has Three Visitors. Sodom and Gomorrah Are Destroyed

Bible Story: Genesis 18:1—19:29

Bible Verse: "For nothing is impossible with God" (Luke 1:37).

Simple Supplies: *You'll need a Bible, a marker or chalk, a sheet of poster board or a chalkboard, a piece of paper, a pen, and an envelope.*

On the poster board, write the following groups of numbers, which form a message the children will decipher. The message is "For nothing is impossible with God."

21 12 9   13 12 7 19 18 13 20   18 8

18 14 11 12 8 8 18 25 15 22   4 18 7 19   20 12 23.

On the piece of paper, write the following code:

A=26	F=21	K=16	P=11	U=6
B=25	G=20	L=15	Q=10	V=5
C=24	H=19	M=14	R=9	W=4
D=23	I=18	N=13	S=8	X=3
E=22	J=17	O=12	T=7	Y=2
				Z=1

Before the sermon, set up the poster board or chalkboard so everyone can see it. Place the paper with the code on it in the envelope, and place the envelope in a pocket or in your Bible.

As children come forward, look at the poster board as if you're trying to decipher its message. I'm so glad you're here today! I really need your help. Someone left me this note, and I can't figure it out. Can you help me? *Pause for a minute while children look at the poster board and try to figure it out.* You know, we need a code or something to help us. Hey, wait a minute! I forgot to look in the envelope that was also left with this message. *Show kids the envelope, and take out the code.* Oh, this should help. Each number goes with a letter! Let's see if we can figure out the message now. *Let older children write the corresponding letters under the numbers on the poster board. When they've finished, read aloud the message.* What an interesting message! The code made it possible for us to figure out the message. In the same way, God makes *anything* possible because—just as the message says—nothing is impossible with God!

In the book of Genesis in the Bible, we learn about some people who found out that nothing is impossible with God. One day God sent some visitors to a man named Abraham to tell him that his wife, Sarah, was going to have a baby. Do you know what Sarah did when she heard the news? *Pause for children to respond.* Sarah laughed. You see, Abraham and Sarah were even older than your grandparents. Can you imagine your grandparents having a new baby? Does that seem funny to you and make you want to laugh? *Lead children in laughing.* Sarah laughed because she thought it was impossible for her to have a baby. But what does our message say? *Open your Bible to Luke 1:37, and show the page to the children.*

Luke 1:37 says, **"For nothing is impossible with God."** Sarah was too old to have a baby, but God made it possible.

Abraham and Sarah weren't the only ones who found out that nothing is impossible with God. Two towns called Sodom and Gomorrah were full of people who did a lot of bad things. The people were so harmful to others that God decided to destroy the cities. But do you know what? People didn't believe that God could destroy the cities; they thought it was a joke. Everybody, stand up and pretend that I am God. When I say to you that I will destroy your cities, laugh as hard as you can. Here we go. *Say the following in the deepest, sternest voice you can:* I will destroy your cities. *Encourage children to laugh hysterically. In a couple of moments, ask them to be seated.* The people thought it was impossible for God to destroy the cities, but what does our message say? *Allow children to respond.*

"**For nothing is impossible with God.**" God can do anything!

The really incredible thing is that God can *still* do anything. No problem you have is too big for God. All you have to do is ask God for help and then believe he will help. Remember, **"nothing is impossible with God."**

Let's pray. Dear God, thank you for making everything possible with you. Help us to look to you for help, and help us believe that you will help. In Jesus' name, amen.

Isaac Is Born

Bible Story: Genesis 21:1-6

> **Bible Verse:** "Rejoice in the Lord always. I will say it again: Rejoice!" (Philippians 4:4).

Simple Supplies: *You'll need a Bible, cookies, napkins, and a doll. Instead of using a doll, you could ask a parent to bring up a real infant.*

hat's something you really, really want? *Choose a few children to share.* Well, I brought something today you might want. I brought some cookies! But you'll have to wait until the end of the children's sermon to get a cookie. When else have you had to wait a long time for something you really wanted? *Choose a few different children to share.* You've had to wait for things you want, so you know how Sarah, a woman in the Bible, felt.

Sarah really, really wanted a baby. But Sarah had to wait a long, long, long time. She had to wait until she was older than most of your grandparents! Then God promised that she'd have a baby. What do you think Sarah did when she heard she was going to have a baby at such an old age? *Pause.* Sarah laughed! But God kept his promise, as he always does, and Sarah did have a baby. Do you know what she did after she had the baby? *Pause.* She laughed again! Everyone, turn to someone next to you and make a silly face. *As children make silly faces, laugh.* It's a lot of fun to laugh. Do you know why Sarah laughed after she had the baby? *Pause.* Sarah was so happy to have a baby that she laughed for joy!

I brought a friend with me today. *Show children the doll, or ask the parent to bring up the infant.* It's a baby. Isn't the baby beautiful? Do any of you have a baby at your house? *Pause.* New babies cause a lot of excitement. Why do you think babies are so exciting? *Pause. Pass the doll around or allow children to see the baby.* What are some other things you're joyful or happy about? *Pause.*

I want to read a verse from the Bible to you. *Open your Bible to Philippians 4:4, and show the page to the children.*

Philippians 4:4 says, **"Rejoice in the Lord always. I will say it again: Rejoice!"** Babies are one of the great things God gives us, and that's why we rejoice. What does it mean to rejoice? *Pause.* What other great things does God give us? *Pause.* When God gives us great things, we like to tell him thank you. That's why we rejoice. Sarah laughed and rejoiced when she had a baby after waiting for so long. We can rejoice, too, when God gives us great things.

Let's take time now to rejoice and to thank God for what he's given us. Let's stand up, raise our hands in the air, and shout, "Rejoice in the Lord!" Then we'll take turns thanking God for things he's given us. After each thing, we'll shout, "Rejoice in the Lord" again. Ready? *Lead kids in shouting the phrase, and choose kids to name things they're thankful for. Then close the prayer with the following sentence.* God, we rejoice that you give us so many good things. Thank you for all you do. In Jesus' name, amen.

Remember how I promised you each a cookie? You've waited a long time, though not quite as long as Sarah waited for a baby! *Hand each child a cookie on a napkin as they go back to their seats.*

God Cares for Hagar and Ishmael

Bible Story: Genesis 21:8-21

> **Bible Verse:** "So I say to you: Ask and it will be given to you; seek and you will find; knock and the door will be opened to you" (Luke 11:9).

Simple Supplies: *You'll need a Bible, small pretzel sticks or another salty snack, a pitcher of water, small paper cups, a large cardboard box,*

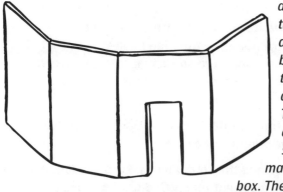

a marker, and scissors. Use the cardboard box to make a door that stands on its own but that you can reach through. First cut the top and bottom from the box. Then cut the box along one of its sides so the box can stand on its own. Use a bold marker to draw a door on the box. Then cut along the door, leaving the "hinge" side connected. Also ask an adult volunteer to help you pour water during the sermon.

Let's begin today with a few quick questions. They may seem silly at first. How did you get into this room today? How do you get into your house? How do you get into your bedroom? *Pause for children to respond.* That's right! You walk through the doors. But what would you do if the door was locked and you didn't have a key? *Pause.* If you knocked on a locked door, what do you think would happen? *Pause.* Oh, I see. If you knock on a door, someone will open it for you.

That kind of reminds me of the Bible story about Hagar and her son, Ishmael. Hagar and Ishmael were wandering in the desert, and they had run out of water. They were getting thirstier and thirstier. Let's play a game to see what that might have been like. *Give each child a small pretzel stick. As kids eat, bring out the pitcher of water and cups so children can see them. Then set the cardboard door in front of the water.*

After kids have finished eating their pretzels, have them begin walking in a circle. After that salty treat, let's pretend we're wandering in the desert like Hagar and Ishmael. Without saying anything, show me how you might feel as I describe the desert. But remember, keep wandering!

Have fun "hamming it up" as you offer the following descriptions. You may want to lead kids in actions such as pretending to protect their eyes from the sun, hopping as if on hot sand, and clutching their dry throats. Pause between sentences to give children time to act out your descriptions. The sun is so, so bright, and the sand is so, so hot. Your mouth is getting so, so dry. Boy, are you thirsty! What you really need is a drink of water. But there's no water in the desert, is there? The sun is getting hotter and hotter. You're so thirsty and so tired. You can hardly keep going. If only you had some water! *Have children kneel and crawl in the circle.* You're so thirsty you can barely crawl anymore. Where will you ever find water in this desert? Finally you can't go on. You're so thirsty you just fall down in the sand.

Have children stay just as they are as you ask the following questions. Let kids call out answers as they lie in the "desert." If this really were the desert and you really were dying of thirst, what would you do right now? You'd ask for a drink of water? But there's a door between you and the water. What would you do? One by one, crawl over, and show me how you'd knock on the door and ask for water.

Let children take turns knocking on the cardboard door and asking for a drink of water. Have your volunteer pour small cups of water and, as each child knocks on the door and asks for a drink of water, open the door and hand a cup of water through. After each child has received a cup of water, have him or her move away from the box and sit down.

In our game, you wandered and wandered looking for water, but the water was there all the time. All you had to do was knock on the door and ask for it. In the same way, Hagar and Ishmael wandered in the desert and cried to God for help. God heard them and gave them the water they needed. *Open your Bible to Luke 11:9, and show the page to the children.*

Listen to what the Bible says in Luke 11:9 about asking God for help: **"So I say to you: Ask and it will be given to you; seek and you will find; knock and the door will be opened to you."**

In our game, you received water when you knocked on the door and asked for it. In our Bible story, God gave Hagar and Ishmael what they needed. God will give us what we need, too. When we knock on God's door, he'll always answer. Let's thank God for being so good to us.

 Dear God, thank you for always answering the door when we knock. And thank you for always listening when we ask for help. Thank you for loving us. In Jesus' name, amen.

Give children each another pretzel stick before they head back to their seats. As you eat this salty pretzel stick, remember that God is always ready to answer the door. All you have to do is knock!

SECTION
TWO

WINTER
QUARTER

John the Baptist Prepares the Way for Jesus

Bible Story: Mark 1:1-8

> **Bible Verse:** "Create in me a pure heart, O God, and renew a steadfast spirit within me" (Psalm 51:10).

Simple Supplies: *You'll need a Bible, a sponge, a bowl of water, and noisemakers.*

Have any of you ever been to a birthday party? What did you have to do to get ready to go? Wait, don't answer me! I'd like you to act out some things you might do to get ready for a party. *Encourage children to act out what they do to get ready for a party.* Wow, it looks as if you've gotten ready for a lot of parties!

How would you get ready for a party if you knew Jesus was going to be there? *Pause for children to respond.* It'd be great to share Jesus with our friends at a party, wouldn't it?

I'd like to tell you about a man called John the Baptist. He knew Jesus was coming to earth, and John wanted the people to be ready to meet Jesus. The Bible says people from all over the countryside went to hear John speak. He told them that Jesus was coming, and he told them what to do to get ready for Jesus.

What do you think people needed to do to get ready for Jesus? *Pause.* Let's hear what John told the people. After I speak, I'd like all of you sitting here to respond, "Let's get ready!" Then, after you, the children, have responded, I'd like the congregation to say, "Let's get ready!" *Be sure everyone understands their roles.* Here we go!

Hey, everybody! We need to get ready for Jesus! *Pause for children and then the congregation to respond.* Hey, all you people! You've done bad things! *Pause for the children and then the congregation to respond.* Hey, everyone! God will forgive you if you ask him to! *Pause for the children and then the congregation to respond.* Great job, everyone!

John helped people understand that to get ready for Jesus, they needed to ask God to forgive them for their sins, or the wrong things they'd done. You know, all of us have done wrong things, but God forgives us when we ask him to. *Open the Bible to Psalm 51:10, and show the page to the children.* Psalm 51:10 says, **"Create in me a pure heart, O God, and renew a steadfast spirit within me."** This means God's forgiveness cleans our hearts and helps us not to do wrong things.

Let's ask God to forgive us for the wrong things we've done. *Have children gather in a circle close to you and each hold out a hand.* I'd like you to close your eyes, and think about a wrong thing you've done. Maybe you fought with a brother or sister, or maybe you didn't do something a parent asked you to do. One by one, I'm going to wash your hands. As I wash your hand, you can say, "God, please forgive me." *Wash children's hands, and help them respond. If a child chooses not to respond, that's OK. Close the prayer with the following:*

Dear God, thank you for John the Baptist, who prepared the way for Jesus by helping people ask for forgiveness. And God, thank you so much for forgiving us, for cleaning sin from our hearts. In Jesus' name, amen.

Just as I cleaned your hand, God cleaned your heart when you asked him to forgive you. Now we're ready to meet Jesus, so let's celebrate! *Distribute noisemakers, and encourage children to sound them and cheer. Collect the noisemakers before you send children back to their seats.*

God Dwells With Us

Bible Story: John 1:1-14

> **Bible Verse:** "The Word became flesh and made his dwelling among us. We have seen his glory, the glory of the One and Only, who came from the Father, full of grace and truth" (John 1:14).

Simple Supplies: *You'll need a Bible and a plastic hand mirror.*

As you make your way toward me, think about what you look like. When you get here, I'll let you look in my mirror to see what you look like. *Let children take turns looking at themselves in the hand mirror; as they do, repeat the question, "What do you look like?"*

What color eyes did you see in the mirror? what hairstyle? What facial expressions did you see—smiles or frowns, for example? What else did you see? *Pause for children to respond.* All the things you named about your eyes, hair, and facial expressions tell what you look like. The mirror can also show us how we act; we can see ourselves waving hello or hugging a friend.

Did you know that Jesus is like a mirror? When we look at Jesus, we see how God acts; that helps us know who God is. For example, when we look in the Bible and see Jesus helping someone, we know God cares for people.

When Jesus came to earth, he showed us who God is. *Open your Bible to John 1:14, and show the page to the children.* John 1:14 says, **"The Word became flesh and made his dwelling among us. We have seen his glory, the glory of the One and Only, who came from the Father, full of grace and truth."** This means Jesus came to live on earth so we could see God and know what God is like.

Let's see how Jesus is like a mirror. Choose a partner, and act out how Jesus might treat that person. For example, you might pretend to help each other, pretend to heal each other, or hug each other. Then we'll think about what that action shows us about God. *Encourage children to form pairs and act out how Jesus might treat their partners. Point out what a few pairs are doing.* What do [children's names] actions tell us about God? *Pause.* Those were wonderful actions! They taught us about God.

Jesus came to earth and showed us who God is. Let's pass around the mirror and take turns thanking God for sending Jesus and for showing us what he's like. You might say, "God, thank you for sending Jesus," "God, we like knowing you," or "God, thank you for showing us who you are." *Begin the prayer. Then pass around the mirror, and help children who want to pray.* Amen. *Hold up the mirror.* How is Jesus like a mirror? *Pause.* Jesus shows us what God is like.

Jesus Is Born

Bible Story: Luke 1:26-38; 2:1-20

Bible Verses: "Do not be afraid. I bring you good news of great joy that will be for all the people. Today in the town of David a Savior has been born to you; he is Christ the Lord" (Luke 2:10b-11).

Simple Supplies: *You'll need a Bible, a candle, matches, and two adult volunteers. Before the sermon, ask one volunteer to approach you at the very beginning of the children's sermon and whisper in your ear. Ask the other volunteer to play the role of the angel. Have the "angel" read what he or she is to say and carry a lit candle while speaking the lines.*

As children gather around you, have an adult volunteer whisper into *your ear.* Oh, I just received a message about some good news. We often get messages, don't we, when we need to know good news? We might hear the good news on the TV or get a telephone call. Well, when a woman named Mary needed to know about some good news, an angel visited her. And the message I just received said we're going to hear what that angel said to Mary. *Have the "angel" volunteer stand facing the children and the congregation and say the following:* "Mary! Mary! I have good news for you! You're going to have a baby! And there's more: Your baby will be called God's own Son, and he will change the world forever!" *The angel may depart at this point.* Wow! What an amazing piece of good news for Mary. And just as the angel said, Mary did have a baby. Isn't that good news?

Tell me about some good news you've had. Maybe your mom had a baby, you earned a good grade, or you found something you lost. Every time someone tells us their good news, let's all jump up and down and shout, "Hooray! That's good news!" Ready? Let's stand up. *Choose several children to share. Each time, lead kids in jumping up and down and shouting. Afterward, have kids sit down again.* Wow, that's all wonderful news!

We like to share our good news with others, don't we? And we like to hear good news, too. Well, Jesus' birth was the best news ever, and God wanted to share that news. Do you know how God shared the good news about Jesus' birth? He sent a whole bunch of angels to tell a group of shepherds about Jesus' birth. Let's read from the Bible to learn what the angel said. *Open your Bible to Luke 2:10b-11, and show the page to the children.* In Luke 2:10b-11, the angel said to the shepherds, **"Do not be afraid. I bring you good news of great joy that will be for all the people. Today in the town of David a Savior has been born to you; he is Christ the Lord."**

Let's pretend we're angels who want to tell everyone the good news about Jesus' birth. Let's go out into the congregation. I want each of you to tell three people, "Good news! Jesus is born!" Can you say that? *Practice the lines with the kids.* OK, let's each tell three people the good news and then come back here. *Send kids into the congregation. You may want to walk with the younger children to help them. After a minute, call the kids back.* Now everyone—including the congregation—say together, "Good news! Jesus is born!" *Lead everyone in saying the good news.* That's great! It's fun to share good news.

If an angel came to tell you the good news of a baby's birth, what do you think you'd do? *Pause.* Well, the shepherds were so excited about the good news that they hurried to find the baby, and they told everyone what had happened.

Jesus' birth was the best news ever. Let's show God how glad we are about the good news of Jesus' birth by singing a prayer to worship him. Let's all—congregation included—sing the first verse of "Joy to the World!" *Lead the children and congregation in the song.*

Joy to the world! The Lord has come!
Let earth receive her king!
Let ev'ry heart prepare him room.
And heav'n and nature sing. And heav'n and nature sing.
And heav'n and heav'n and nature sing.

faithful People Thank God for Jesus

Bible Story: Luke 2:22-40

Bible Verse: "Enter his gates with thanksgiving and his courts with praise; give thanks to him and praise his name" (Psalm 100:4).

Simple Supplies: *You'll need a Bible, plastic drinking straws, scissors, a small trash bag, and an adult volunteer. Cut the drinking straws so that you have three groups of straws, each group smaller than the previous group. You'll need one piece of straw for each child.*

As children come toward you, display the straw pieces. Everyone, choose a piece of straw. You can have a short piece, a medium piece, or a long piece. *Let each child choose.* Now I'm going to walk to the other side of the room. *Walk to one side of the room, and ask the adult volunteer to stay with the children. Wait for fifteen seconds.* Now those of you who have a short piece of straw can join me. *As children join you, whisper to each child something nice about himself or herself—"You're so nice" or "You're such a great helper," for example.* Now those of you who have a medium piece of straw can join me. *Again, whisper to each child that joins you something nice about himself or herself.* Now those of you who have the longest pieces of straw can join me. I've told the others something nice about themselves, and now I'll tell you something nice, too. *Whisper to each child that joins you something nice about himself or herself.*

Was it easy or difficult to wait to join us? Why? What did you like about what happened when you finally got here? *Pause for children to respond.* It's hard to wait sometimes, but it's great when something nice happens after a long wait. What's the best thing you've had to wait for? *Pause.* Those are great things!

In the Bible, some people had to wait a long, long time for something even better. They had to wait for Jesus to come to earth. One man named Simeon waited his whole life to see Jesus. Finally Jesus was born. How do you feel when something you've been waiting a long time for finally happens? *Pause.* It's very exciting, isn't it? Well, Simeon was very excited when he finally saw baby Jesus. Do you know what Simeon did? He praised God for Jesus and for letting him see Jesus. Let's clap and cheer to show how excited Simeon was to see Jesus. *Lead children in clapping and cheering.* A woman named Anna was also excited to see baby Jesus because she knew he was going to change the world. Do you know what she did? She thanked God for Jesus and told other people that he was the one they had been waiting for. Let's clap and cheer again to show how happy Anna was to see Jesus. *Lead children in clapping and cheering.*

When something great happens, like Jesus' birth, it's great to thank God as Simeon and Anna did. *Open your Bible to Psalm 100:4, and show the page to the children.* Psalm 100:4 says, **"Enter his gates with**

thanksgiving and his courts with praise; give thanks to him and praise his name." This means we should praise and thank God for good things just as Simeon and Anna did.

Why don't we praise and thank God now for good things in our lives. Maybe you'd even like to thank God for Jesus just as Simeon and Anna did. *Hold up the trash bag.* Bring your pieces of straw to me, and put them in this bag. As you do, say one thing you'd like to thank God for. *Begin the prayer by saying something you're thankful for, and then encourage each child to put the piece of straw in the bag and say what he or she is thankful for. It's OK if a child chooses not to say anything. Afterward, close the prayer with the following:* Thank you, God, for everything you do for us. Thank you especially for Jesus. Amen. Now, as you go back to your seats, let's cheer and clap one more time to show how thankful we are to God. *Lead children in clapping and cheering.*

Wise Men find Jesus

Bible Story: Matthew 2:1-12

> **Bible Verse:** "Enter his gates with thanksgiving and his courts with praise; give thanks to him and praise his name" (Psalm 100:4).

Simple Supplies: *You'll need a Bible, a basket, and pennies.*

I'd like to tell you a story. This isn't a true story; it's only make-believe. As I tell you this story, I'd like you to act out certain parts. Just do as I do.

Once upon a time, there was a boy named Nathan No-thanks. Nathan No-thanks never said thank you for anything. His mom fixed meals, and Nathan dove right into his food without ever saying thank you. *Lead children in pretending to eat.* Nathan's dad helped him get ready for soccer games, but Nathan ran out the door with his soccer ball without saying thank you. *Lead children in pretending to kick a ball.* Many people helped Nathan, but he never said thank you.

One day Nathan's whole family came for dinner. Both of his grandmas were there, plus his favorite uncle, and even the cousin he saw only once a year. Before they began to eat, Nathan's mom did something unusual. She said, "Let's tell Jesus what we're thankful for." Nathan began to get nervous. "Thankful?" he wondered to himself. "I don't need to be thankful for anything."

One of Nathan's favorite aunts began to talk. The more she spoke, the more nervous he became. He began to make a sad face. *Lead children in making sad faces.* Then as Nathan's dad spoke, Nathan started to whimper. *Lead kids in whimpering.* Soon Nathan was so nervous that he began to whine. *Lead children in whining.* Then he began to cry. *Lead children in crying.* Then Nathan totally lost control and began to sob loudly. *Lead children in sobbing loudly.*

Nathan's mom put her arm around him. She asked, "Nathan, why are you crying?" Nathan cried, "I don't have anything to be thankful for. I don't even *want* to be thankful!" So Nathan's mom told him that a long, long time ago, some very wise men knew a king had been born. They knew the baby would grow up to be a great king, so they wanted to give thanks for him. They searched and searched and traveled very far until they found the baby, whose name was Jesus. These very wise men were so happy to find baby Jesus that they bowed down, worshipped him, and gave him expensive gifts. Nathan's mom explained that everything good in the world comes from God and that's why we should thank God as the wise men did. Then Nathan's mom showed him a verse from the Bible. I'd like to show that verse to you. *Open the Bible to Psalm 100:4, and show the page to the children.* Psalm 100:4 says, **"Enter his gates with thanksgiving and his courts with praise; give thanks to him and praise his name."** God wants us to come to him with all kinds of thanks for the things he's given us.

What do you think happened to Nathan? *Pause for children to respond.* Nathan spent ten minutes telling everyone what he was thankful for. When he was finished, he leapt for joy because it felt so good to thank God. Let's all shout, "Thank you, God!" and leap for joy, too. *Lead children in shouting and leaping for joy.*

In the story Nathan's mom told, the wise men gave gifts to Jesus. I'd like us to do that today. *Distribute the pennies, then hold up the basket.* I'm going to pass around this basket, and I'd like you to place your coin in the basket and say one thing you're thankful for. *Pass the basket, and allow children to share. Close the prayer with the following:* Dear God, thank you so much for Jesus and for all the good things you give us. Amen.

John Baptizes Jesus

Bible Story: Mark 1:4-11

> **Bible Verse:** "For God so loved the world that he gave his one and only Son, that whoever believes in him shall not perish but have eternal life" (John 3:16).

Simple Supplies: *You'll need a Bible.*

Let's start today by singing a song for everyone. When you've finished, I'll bet the congregation will clap and cheer for you! Let's sing "Jesus Loves Me." *Lead kids in singing "Jesus Loves Me" or another song of your choice. Afterward, lead the congregation in clapping and cheering for the children.*

Wow, it sure is fun to hear people clap and cheer for you, isn't it? Why do you think the congregation just clapped and cheered for us? *Pause for children to respond.* It's nice for the congregation to tell us they like to hear us sing. I'd like a couple of you to tell me or even show me other things you can do well. *Choose a few children to share their talents with everyone.* That's wonderful! Let's all clap for [child's name]. *Lead children in clapping.*

Another great thing you can all do is show God you love him. When we show God we love him, he's pleased with us, just as we were pleased to see and hear about all your wonderful talents. In the Bible, John the Baptist told people how to show their love to God. John said we need to tell God we're sorry for the wrong things we do. Now let's all close our eyes for just a moment and tell God we're sorry about a wrong thing we've done. I'll start our prayer, and then we can all silently pray to God. Let's pray. Dear God, we're sorry for doing these wrong things. Please forgive us. *Pause for a moment of silent prayer. Then close the prayer with the following:* Thank you, God, for loving us and forgiving us. In Jesus' name, amen.

John baptized the people who told God they were sorry and would try to do better. John also told the people that someone great was coming to help them know God even better. Do you know who that someone was? *Pause.* It was Jesus! Of course, Jesus wanted to show his love for

God, so he went to be baptized by John, too. Remember how pleased everyone was when you sang? Well, when Jesus was baptized, God was very pleased with him. Can you tell me about a time someone was proud of you? *Choose a few children to share.* I'm proud of all of you for being here today. How does it make you feel when people are proud of you? *Pause.* It feels great to do things that make others proud of us. When John baptized Jesus, God was so proud of Jesus that he said, "You are my Son, whom I love; with you I am well pleased."

We can also please God and show him how much we love him by be-lieving in Jesus. *Open your Bible to John 3:16, and show the page to the children.* John 3:16 says, **"For God so loved the world that he gave his one and only Son, that whoever believes in him shall not perish but have eternal life."** That means when we believe in Jesus, God is so pleased with us that we can live with him forever in heaven. Isn't that wonderful?

Let's sing "Jesus Loves Me" again. This time, sing it for God to show him how much you love him and his Son, Jesus. *Lead kids in singing "Je-sus Loves Me." Then encourage the congregation to applaud again be-fore dismissing the children.*

Jesus Surprises Nathanael

Bible Story: John 1:43-51; Psalm 139:1-6, 13-18

> **Bible Verses:** "O Lord, you have searched me and you know me. You know when I sit and when I rise; you perceive my thoughts from afar. You discern my going out and my lying down; you are familiar with all my ways" (Psalm 139:1-3).

Simple Supplies: *You'll need a Bible, a pen, three Styrofoam cups, a marble or other small object, a tray, and a sonogram picture of a devel-oping baby (if available). Before the sermon, mark a small dot on a cup. Try to make it visible to you and only you. Place the three cups upside down on the tray.*

L et's start our time together with a game. I have three cups and a marble. I'll place the marble under a cup and move the cups about, and then we'll guess where the marble is. *Place the marble under the cup with the dot on it. Move the cups about, and have kids guess where the marble is. Walk around with the tray so all the kids have a chance to see the cups. Let one or two children move the cups about so you can "guess" where the marble is. After a minute, set the tray out of children's reach.* Why do you think I always knew where the marble was? *Pause for children to respond.* Well, I had a helper. *Show children the mark on the cup.* This mark made it easy for me to find the marble. Did you know that just as I always knew where the marble was, God always knows where you are and what you're doing? In fact, God knows everything about you.

Open your Bible to Psalm 139:1-3, and show the page to the children. Psalm 139:1-3 says, **"O Lord, you have searched me and you know me. You know when I sit and when I rise; you perceive my thoughts from afar. You discern my going out and my lying down; you are familiar with all my ways."** God loves you so much that he has learned all about you.

Did you know that God knew all of these neat things about you before you were even born? *Show the sonogram picture of the developing baby if you have one.* This is a picture of a baby in the mother's tummy. God already knows all about this baby. God knows how many hairs are going to be on this baby's head, what the baby will look like as a grown-up, and even who this baby's friends will be. Everyone, look at your arm. Try to count the number of hairs you see on your arm. *Allow some time for children to do this. For children who can't yet count, you may want to count aloud as you count the hairs on your arm.* Wow! We can't even count all the hairs on our arms, but God knows just how many hairs you have. And God knows *everything* about us! Isn't that amazing?

Jesus showed us how well God knows us. Once Jesus amazed a man named Nathanael, who didn't understand why his friends thought Jesus was so special. Nathanael didn't even want to meet Jesus. But when Nathanael finally met Jesus, Jesus told Nathanael he had seen what Nathanael was doing and knew Nathanael before they had even met. Do you think we can do that? I'm going to close my eyes, and I want you to make a face or strike a pose. Then I'm going to try to guess what you're doing. *Close your eyes, try to guess what a few children are doing, and laugh as you fail.* I can't see what you're doing, but Jesus could see what Nathanael was doing. As you can imagine, Nathanael began to understand why Jesus is so special!

Just as Jesus knew about Nathanael, God knows all about you. He knew all about you before you were even born, and he knows all about you now. God has known us, and loved us, from the beginning of time. Let's thank God for loving us and knowing us so well. Dear God, thank you for loving us so much that you know all about us. In Jesus' name, amen.

Disciples follow Jesus

Bible Story: Mark 1:14-20

> **Bible Verse:** " 'Come, follow me,' Jesus said, 'and I will make you fishers of men' " (Mark 1:17).

Simple Supplies: *You'll need a Bible, a stick, a three-foot piece of string, a clothespin, a bucket, sandwich-sized plastic bags, and ginger-bread men cookies. Before the sermon, tie the string to the stick, and attach the clothespin to the loose end of the string. For each child, place one cookie in a plastic bag, and place the cookies in the bucket.*

As children come forward, toss the fishing line toward the congregation. Hey, everyone! We're going on a fishing trip today. I've already begun to fish, but I just can't seem to get a fish to bite. Would any of you like to try to catch a fish today? *Place the bucket full of cookies so the children can face the congregation as they "fish." Have one child fish by casting the string into the bucket. Attach a bag with a cookie in it to the clothespin.* Wow! Look at that! You caught a...what is that? It's a gingerbread man. *Allow every child who wants to fish to do so. Distribute cookies to any children who don't want to fish. Instruct kids to set aside their cookies for later.*

Did you know that Jesus liked to go

43

fishing too? We just went fishing for gingerbread men, but Jesus liked to go fishing for real people! Jesus didn't use a stick and a string, though. Instead, he told people about God's love for them. Instead of catching cookies, Jesus caught disciples, or people who helped him tell others about God's love. The Bible tells us how Jesus fished for disciples. One day Jesus saw two brothers, and he called to them. He asked them to be his disciples, learn from him, and tell others about God's love. This is what Jesus said to the brothers. *Open your Bible to Mark 1:17, and show the* *page to the children.* Mark 1:17 says, **"'Come, follow me,' Jesus said, 'and I will make you fishers of men.'"** Jesus needed the brothers to help him be fishers by telling others about God's love.

Do you know what those brothers did when Jesus asked them to follow him? Right away, they left their things and followed Jesus. Who is your hero, your favorite sports figure, or your favorite movie star? Would you want to leave your family, your home, and all of your things behind to follow that person everywhere? *Pause for children to respond.* Well, that's what the brothers did. They could tell that Jesus was more special than anyone in the world—even more special than the heroes you just named. The brothers and the other disciples were excited to follow Jesus and to be fishers by telling others about God's love.

We can be fishers, too, by telling others about God's love. How do you think you can tell others about God's love? *Pause.* Those are wonderful ideas! Let's tell everyone here today about God's love right now. I'm going to count to three, and then we'll shout, "God loves you!" to the congregation. Ready? One, two, three—God loves you! What a wonderful way to tell others about God's love.

 Let's thank God for letting us fish for people. Dear God, thank you for asking us to be your fishers. Help us as we try to tell others about your love. In Jesus' name, amen. Don't forget to take your gingerbread men home. As you eat them, think about how you can be one of Jesus' fishers.

Jesus Demonstrates His Authority

Bible Story: Mark 1:21-28

> **Bible Verses:** "For I am convinced that neither death nor life, neither angels nor demons, neither the present nor the future, nor any powers, neither height nor depth, nor anything else in all creation, will be able to separate us from the love of God that is in Christ Jesus our Lord" (Romans 8:38-39).

Simple Supplies: *You'll need a Bible, and a large paper clip for every child. Choose paper clips that are larger than a quarter so they aren't choking hazards for young children.*

I want to remind you about something very important today: Jesus is always with you, and he always loves you. You might worry about being separated from Jesus, so first let's find out what it means to be separated. I'd like you to sit boy, girl, boy, girl. *Help the children sit boy, girl, boy, girl. If two boys or two girls need to sit next to each other, be sure they sit some distance apart.* Now the boys are separated from the boys, and the girls are separated from the girls. What does it mean to be separated? *Pause for children to respond.* That's right! When we're separated, we're apart from each other. When we're separated, we can't help each other and we can't do fun things together.

The girls are separated, and the boys are separated. But you'll never be separated from Jesus because he has authority. Can you point to some people who have authority over you? These are people who know so much that they can teach you about life and tell you what to do. *Pause.* Your moms and dads, grandmas and grandpas, and teachers may have authority over some people, but Jesus has authority over everyone in the world. Jesus knows so much that he teaches us about God and about how to live. People in the Bible who heard Jesus teach were amazed at how much he knew. Those people also saw how Jesus' authority kept a man from being separated from God. Just as the girls are separated and the boys are separated, the Bible tells about a man who was separated from God by an evil spirit. What do you think it would be like to be separated from God? *Pause.* The good news is that Jesus told the evil spirit to leave the man alone. Because Jesus has authority, the evil spirit did as Jesus said. So Jesus made it possible for the man to be close to God again. Jesus has authority, and he will make sure you are never, ever separated from God.

Let's see what it looks like to be close instead of separated. I'm going to give each of you a paper clip, and then you'll all link your paper clips together to make a long chain. *Distribute the paper clips, and help children link their paper clips together.* Just as these paper clips are connected, Jesus will make sure we're connected to God forever. *Open your Bible to Romans 8:38-39, and show the page to the children.* Romans 8:38-39 says, **"For I am convinced that neither death nor life, neither angels nor demons, neither the present nor the future, nor any powers, neither height nor depth, nor anything else in all creation, will be able to separate us from the love of God that is in Christ Jesus our Lord."** Jesus will let nothing separate you from God—nothing! Let's thank God for that: Dear God, thank you for sending Jesus so we can always be close to you. In Jesus' name, amen.

Jesus Heals, Prays, and Preaches

Bible Story: Mark 1:29-39

 Bible Verse: "Come to me, all you who are weary and burdened, and I will give you rest" (Matthew 11:28).

Simple Supplies: *You'll need a Bible; Band-Aid bandages; and a variety of make-believe hospital or sickroom supplies such as bandages, small blankets, stuffed animals, stethoscopes, and a doctor's bag.*

Have you ever been sick? What was that like? *Choose one or two children to share.* It's not very much fun being sick, is it? Who takes care of you when you're sick? What do they do for you? *Pause.*

There's a story in the Bible about how Jesus healed lots of sick people. He made them well again. Let's pretend some of you are sick and some of you are taking care of the sick people. *Have kids form two groups. Have one group of children pretend they're sick, and let the other group of children use the make-believe supplies to "care" for the sick children.*

After several minutes, call children back together and collect the supplies.

It's nice to have someone care about you and take care of you when you're sick or hurt, isn't it? In the Bible story I mentioned, Jesus made sick people well. But he can do much more than that! Sometimes people can be hurt on the inside, even if no one can see the hurt on the outside. Sometimes people are sad or lonely or upset. And Jesus can take care of those kinds of hurts, too.

Open your Bible to Matthew 11:28, and show the page to the children. Listen to what Jesus says in the Bible: **"Come to me, all you who are weary and burdened, and I will give you rest."** Jesus can heal all of our problems—the inside hurts and the outside hurts.

Think of one inside hurt you have right now. Maybe you're sad because a pet died or your friend moved away or you're having a problem at school. Don't say anything out loud; just think of your problem. I'm going to put a Band-Aid on your hand to help you remember that Jesus can heal all your hurts. *Have children come forward, and place a Band-Aid on each child's hand.*

Our Bible verse says Jesus will give us rest. I want each of you to lie down and put your head on your hands as if you were resting. Then we'll pray together and ask Jesus to help us with the hurts we thought of. *Wait for children to get into resting positions, then pray.* Dear God, thank you so much for taking care of our hurts. Please help these children with the hurts they're thinking of right now. *Pause.* Thank you for loving us and for giving us rest. In Jesus' name, amen.

Every time you look at your Band-Aid today, remember that Jesus loves you and will take care of all of your hurts—the inside ones and the outside ones.

Jesus Calms a Storm

Bible Story: Mark 4:35-41

Bible Verse: "Cast all your anxiety on him because he cares for you" (1 Peter 5:7).

Simple Supplies: *You'll need a Bible.*

Today I'd like all of you to sit in the shape of a boat. *Have kids stand in a circle. Then have kids form two ends so the circle becomes a boat shape. Have kids sit down again.* Do you wonder why you're seated in the shape of a boat? *Open your Bible to 1 Peter 5:7, and show the page to the children.* First Peter 5:7 says, **"Cast all your anxiety on him because he cares for you."** Anxiety is worry or fear. Because Jesus loves us, he wants us to give our anxiety to him. Our boat shape is going to help us practice doing this.

Let's take an imaginary trip to practice giving Jesus our anxiety. Everybody, lean to the right. Now, everybody, lean slowly to the left. Pretend we're in a boat and the waves are rocking us left and right, left and right, left and right. Keep rocking while I tell you a true story from the Bible. Jesus and his disciples were in a boat. The boat gently rocked the disciples just as we are. Then a big storm came. The wind blew! Let's all blow like the wind. *Pause.* The rain fell. Let's pat the floor to sound like the rain. *Pause.* Instead of rocking left and right, the boat pitched every which way in the storm. Let's sway left and right and back and forth. How would you feel if you had been in that boat in the middle of a storm? *Pause.* The disciples were very afraid. Can you make faces that show how afraid the disciples were? *Pause.* What kinds of things make you feel afraid? *Pause for children to respond.*

Do you know what the disciples did when they became afraid? They cast their anxiety on Jesus. Jesus was asleep, even during the storm, but they woke him up and asked him to help them. Then Jesus did an amazing thing. He told the waves to be quiet and still. And the waves obeyed. Let's gently rock to the left and right again, left and right, left and right. How does this feel different from the storm? *Pause.* Just as Jesus helped the disciples when they were anxious, Jesus will help you. Jesus calmed the storm, and he is with you during the storms, or hard parts, of your life. How do you think you can cast your anxiety and fear on Jesus as the disciples did? *Pause.*

When we ask Jesus to help us, he always does. Let's thank him for this. Gently rock to the left and right again as we pray to help us remember how Jesus calms the storms in our lives. Dear God, we're amazed that Jesus can calm storms. Thank you for loving us so much that you take care of the difficult, stormy times in our lives. Help us to remember to cast our anxiety on you. In Jesus' name, amen.

four friends Help a Paralyzed Man

Bible Story: Mark 2:1-12

> **Bible Verse:** "If we confess our sins, he is faithful and just and will forgive us our sins and purify us from all unrighteousness" (1 John 1:9).

Simple Supplies: *You'll need a Bible, a dry-eraser board or chalkboard, some dry-eraser markers or chalk, an eraser, and one sticker for each child.*

Have you ever wanted to do something so much that you would do almost anything to be able to do it? Tell us what you wanted to do. *Choose a few children to share.* The Bible tells a true story about five men who found a very creative way to do something they wanted to do. You see, Jesus was at a house teaching people. There were so many people in the house that there wasn't room for anyone else. But the five men really, really wanted to see Jesus because one of the men was paralyzed. He couldn't use his arms or legs, and he knew Jesus could help him.

Let's play a game. I have a sticker for each of you, but you have to come get it from me. The catch is that you can't use your legs or arms in any way. Everybody try! *Give kids only a few moments to try because you don't want them to reach you.* Good try, everyone. You can imagine how hard it was for the paralyzed man to get to Jesus. Four of the man's friends carried him to the house to see Jesus, but they couldn't get into the house because of the crowd. So do you know what those men did? *Pause.* That's right. They cut a hole in the roof of the house and lowered the man down to Jesus. What would you do to help a friend get to something they really wanted? *Pause.* You're good friends! What do you think the people in the house thought when they

49

saw this man being lowered from the roof? *Pause.* I think they were pretty shocked and confused. Jesus, however, was calm. When Jesus saw that the men believed he could help the paralyzed man, he said, "Son, your sins are forgiven." What is sin? *Pause.* Let's write some things we've done that we think are sins. *Have each child write something on the board. Help even the young children to scribble on the board.* So when Jesus told the paralyzed man that his sins were forgiven, what did that mean? *Pause.* Jesus erased the man's sins. *Erase all the writing from the board.*

Open your Bible to 1 John 1:9, and show the page to the children. First John 1:9 says, **"If we confess our sins, he is faithful and just and will forgive us our sins and purify us from all unrighteousness."** What does "confess" mean? *Pause.* When we tell, or confess, our sins, God forgives us. When we wrote down our sins, we were confessing. And do you know what God did with those sins, and what he does with all the sins we confess? *Pause.* Yes, God erases them!

But that's not the end of the Bible story. The crowd at the house didn't believe Jesus could forgive sins. So Jesus asked the people if it would be easier to forgive the man's sins or to tell the man to walk. To prove that he had the power to do both, Jesus told the man to get up and walk. The man did! What a miracle! How do you think this made the man feel? *Pause.* Let's pray. Dear God, thank you for forgiving our sins when we tell you we're sorry. Help us to remember to tell you about our sins every day. In Jesus' name, amen.

Remember the stickers I have? Just as the man in the story did, everyone *walk* to me, and I'll give you a sticker. When you look at your sticker, remember that Jesus can erase your sins and help you with your troubles. *Distribute the stickers.*

Jesus Feeds Thousands

Bible Story: John 6:1-15

> **Bible Verse: "And my God will meet all your needs according to his glorious riches in Christ Jesus" (Philippians 4:19).**

Simple Supplies: *You'll need a Bible and fish-shaped crackers.*

What are some things you need to live? *Pause for children to respond.* Jesus cares about us and wants to take care of our needs. A true story from the Bible shows us one way Jesus took care of more than five thousand hungry people. These thousands of people had followed Jesus to hear him teach. The people were hungry, but they didn't have fast-food restaurants like McDonald's or Taco Bell. But Jesus found a way to feed all of them.

One boy had brought a lunch of five small loaves of bread and two small fish. *Hold up the fish-shaped crackers.* Let's pretend these crackers are the bread and fish the boy had. It doesn't look like enough for thousands of people, does it? Well, Jesus thanked God for the boy's lunch and then passed the lunch around. Let's pass around the crackers as the people did. Each of you may take one cracker. *Pass around the package of crackers. You may have children take more crackers depending on the size of your group.* We just have a little taste of cracker, but Jesus used the boy's small lunch to feed thousands of people until they were full! The disciples even gathered twelve baskets of leftovers! This true story teaches us that Jesus can take care of us. *Open your Bible to Philippians 4:19, and show the page to the children.* Philippians 4:19 says, **"And my God will meet all your needs according to his glorious riches in Christ Jesus."**

Jesus used the boy's lunch to feed thousands. In the same way, God often uses people like us to meet the needs of others. How do you think God can use you to help other people? *Pause.* How have other people helped you? *Pause.*

Let's thank God for taking care of us. Dear God, thank you for meeting our needs. Help us to meet other's needs for you. In Jesus' name, amen.

SECTION

THREE

SPRING
QUARTER

Jesus Blesses the Children

Bible Story: Mark 10:13-16

Bible Verse: "Let the little children come to me, and do not hinder them, for the kingdom of God belongs to such as these" (Mark 10:14b).

Simple Supplies: *You'll need a Bible and star-shaped stickers.*

Have you ever heard someone say, "You can't do that; you're too little"? Who wants to tell us about a time someone said that? *Choose a few children to share.* Some of Jesus' disciples felt the same way. People brought their children to Jesus, but the disciples thought the children were too young to talk to Jesus. Well, it's true that children might be too young to do some things, but there are still lots of things you can do. Who wants to show us something you can do? *Choose a few children to share.* Wow, you can do so many neat things! Jesus loves you and knows you can do neat and important things. *Open your Bible to Mark 10:14b, and show the page to the children.* When Jesus' disciples tried to turn the children away, Jesus said, **"Let the little children come to me, and do not hinder them, for the kingdom of God belongs to such as these."** Jesus not only told the disciples not to turn away the children, but even said children can show others how to believe in him. How do you think you can show others how to believe in Jesus? *Pause.* Those are great ideas. You can love Jesus and trust him because he loves you and thinks you're important even though you're young. He hugged the children in the Bible story and blessed them. Let's experience a great big hug like the hug Jesus gave to the children in the Bible story. *Have children form a circle, put their arms around one another, and hug tight.* What do you think it would be like to be hugged by Jesus? *Pause.* Jesus' hug would probably be the best hug in the world.

I'm going to give you a star sticker to remind you that you're a "star" in Jesus' eyes. *Distribute the stickers.* Let's hug again and pray. *Pause.* Dear God, thank you for loving these children, and thank you for the way they show us how to love you. In Jesus' name, amen.

Jesus Heals the Blind Man

Bible Story: Mark 10:46–52

> Bible Verse: "He saved us, not because of righteous things we had done, but because of his mercy" (Titus 3:5a).

Simple Supplies: *You'll need a Bible and a bag of candy.*

L et's start with an experiment. Everybody, close your eyes and cover them with your hands. Tell me what you see. *Pause for children to respond.* How many fingers am I holding up? *Hold up some fingers.* How do you like seeing nothing but darkness? *Pause.* OK, you can take your hands down and open your eyes. Now what do you see? How many fingers am I holding up? *Hold up some fingers.* Which do you like better: the light or the darkness? *Pause.*

The Bible tells a true story about a man who was blind; he couldn't see anything but darkness. Just like you, he wanted to see. He just *knew* Jesus could help him. He went to meet Jesus, but so many people were there. The man couldn't see, remember, so he began shouting for Jesus to have mercy on him.

Can someone tell us what you think the word "mercy" means? *Pause.* I'll try to show you what the word "mercy" means. *Hold up the bag of candy.* I'd love to share this candy with you, but you can have a piece only if you've never watched TV. Raise your hand if you've never watched TV. *Give a piece of candy to anyone who raises a hand. Most likely, children won't raise their hands.* Why aren't you raising your hands? *Pause.* Why don't you all holler "mercy" as the blind man from our Bible story did, and maybe that'll change my mind. *Encourage children to shout for mercy. After a moment, ask them to be quiet again.* OK, because I love you, I'll give you a piece of candy even though you watch TV. *Distribute the candy, but ask kids not to eat it until you've finished the sermon.* This is what it means to show mercy. *Open your Bible to Titus 3:5, and show the page to the children.* Titus 3:5 says, **"He** **saved us, not because of righteous things we had done, but because of his mercy."** This means God forgives us and helps us and saves us not because we've earned it by doing good things, but because he loves us.

Think back to our Bible story about the blind man. He shouted for Jesus to help him. Jesus heard the man and healed him. The man could see! Did the blind man somehow pay for Jesus to heal him? *Pause.* No, the man didn't pay Jesus with money or anything else. The man did nothing to deserve getting his sight back, but Jesus knew that the man loved him. Jesus showed mercy to the man. Jesus treats us the same way. He loves us so much that when we ask him to forgive our sins, he has mercy on us and saves us.

 Let's thank God for his mercy. Dear God, thank you for showing us mercy by saving us even though we don't deserve it. In Jesus' name, amen.

Jesus Teaches About Commitment

Bible Story: Mark 8:31-38

 Bible Verse: "I am not ashamed of the gospel, because it is the power of God for the salvation of everyone who believes: first for the Jew, then for the Gentile" (Romans 1:16).

Simple Supplies: *You'll need a Bible, name tags, and a marker. Before the sermon, create a badge for each child that reads, "I'm not ashamed to tell you about Jesus."*

Today I need your help with something a little silly. Do you mind looking a little silly? I hope not. First I'd like everyone to stand up as straight as you can. *Pause for children to respond.* Great! Now I'd like you to make a fist with each hand and place your hands on your waist. *Demonstrate the posture for children.* Now flap your arms like wings. Do you feel silly yet? Next I'd like you to squat down, and hop around a little. *Demonstrate the posture for children.* Do you feel silly yet? Finally I want you to crow like a rooster. Ready? *Lead children in crowing while bouncing and flapping.* OK, who feels really silly? What's it like to do something silly in front of all these people? *Pause.*

This reminds me of something Jesus talked about in the Bible. Jesus and his disciples, who were his really good friends, were traveling around and teaching people about God. Life was pretty good. But Jesus told his disciples that a time was coming when they would be afraid and ashamed to stick by him. They'd feel as silly about loving Jesus as you felt about acting like a rooster. Can you imagine feeling silly about loving Jesus? *Pause.* Jesus said that instead of being ashamed, he wants us to stick by him no matter what other people do.

Do you know what it means to be ashamed? Being ashamed means we feel sorry or even silly about believing in Jesus. Show me how you act when you're embarrassed or ashamed. *Lead kids in covering their faces, slouching, or trying to hide.* Now show me how you act when you're not ashamed? *Lead kids in standing up straight, smiling, and looking straight ahead.* I want to read to you what one person said about being ashamed of Jesus. *Open your Bible to Romans 1:16, and show the page to the children.* Romans 1:16 says, **"I am not ashamed of the gospel, because it is the power of God for the salvation of everyone who believes: first for the Jew, then for the Gentile."** Being ashamed of Jesus is like saying, "God is powerful and can make people happy, but I'm not going to tell people about him." Now that would be silly! Jesus wants us to tell others about him instead of hiding that we believe in him.

Let's ask God to give us strength to not feel silly for loving Jesus. Dear God, thank you so much for sending Jesus to teach us about life with you. Help us to always stick by Jesus no matter what other people think. Instead of hiding our love for Jesus, help us to tell people about you. In Jesus' name, amen.

Now to show we can be brave instead of afraid, let's crow like roosters one more time. *Lead kids in crowing.* Great job! I have a badge for you that reads, "I'm not ashamed to tell you about Jesus." I'd like you to wear the badge today so you can remember to stick by Jesus. *Distribute the badges.*

Jesus Clears Merchants from the Temple

Bible Story: John 2:13-22

> **Bible Verse:** "Come, let us bow down in worship, let us kneel before the Lord our Maker" (Psalm 95:6).

Simple Supplies: *You'll need a Bible and construction paper.*

*O*pen your Bible to Psalm 95:6, and show the page to the children. Psalm 95:6 says, **"Come, let us bow down in worship, let us kneel before the Lord our Maker."** Worship is a really difficult thing to understand. You can't see it. You can't always hear it. It's hard to tell if people are doing it. But worship is important. Jesus even got upset when people used the temple, a special church, for things other than worship. Let's find out more about worship.

Distribute a piece of construction paper to each child. Make a telescope from your piece of paper by rolling it into a tube and looking at me through it. *Pause for children to create "telescopes," and encourage older children to help the younger ones.* Now sit so you can see my whole face, and only my face, through your telescope. *Pause.* You've just learned the first principle of worship—focus. You focus on God by giving him all your attention. You can do this by using your telescope to look right at a teacher, song leader, or other worship leader. Then you'll find it easier to hear what they say and to focus on God. How else can you focus on God? *Pause for children to respond.* Those are great ideas!

Now use your telescope to look around. What do we do in this room to help us worship God? *Pause.* We worship God in this room by singing and praying and reading the Bible. Every time we come into this room, we can remember that we worship God in this room.

In Jesus' time, the temple was a special place in which people worshipped God. But some people set up tables to sell worship items. They didn't want to worship God; they wanted to make money. Jesus saw what they were doing and turned over their tables. He told those people to leave.

Finally use your telescopes to look at the people in this place. These people are your family members, your neighbors, and your teachers. They can help you focus on God. They are focusing on God themselves. How can these people help you? *Pause.* These people can show you how to worship. They can pray. They can sing. They can focus on God.

Now use your telescope to focus on a cross. *Point to a cross or something similar in the room.* As we pray, use your telescope to help you focus on God by looking at the cross. Dear God, help us focus on you and worship you well. In Jesus' name, amen. Take your telescopes with you to help you focus on God and worship him.

Jesus Explains Why God Sent Him

Bible Story: John 3:13-21

> **Bible Verse: "For God so loved the world that he gave his one and only Son, that whoever believes in him shall not perish but have eternal life" (John 3:16).**

Simple Supplies: *You'll need a Bible, a flashlight, three squares of poster board or newsprint, and a marker. Before the sermon, write the following statements on consecutive pieces of poster board: "Jesus is the light of the world," "Jesus saves us," and "People who believe in Jesus live forever with him in heaven." Station three volunteers around the room to hold up the signs, and give the volunteer with the first sign the flashlight. Also ask a volunteer to turn off the lights on your cue.*

Today I've got some important stuff to tell you about. Let's huddle close so I can tell you about it. *Huddle with the children, being especially sure to sit next to the younger children.* I want to tell you what Jesus once told a man named Nicodemus. *Have the volunteer turn off the lights.* Oh no! It's going to be difficult to tell you the story without any lights. Hey, I remembered my flashlight! But I left it on the other side of the room. Let's walk together to get it. *Encourage children to hold hands as you walk to the first sign.* How does it feel to walk in the darkness? *Pause for children to respond.*

OK, here's my flashlight, and I left it next to an important sign. *Shine the flashlight on the sign.* Jesus told Nicodemus that people were lost as if they were walking around in the dark—just as we were. Jesus said he is the light the world needs. How is Jesus like this flashlight? *Pause.* Why do you think the world needs Jesus? *Pause.* We need God, and Jesus shows us the way to God just as this flashlight shows us the way around the room. Let's keep walking. *Lead children to the sheet that reads, "Jesus saves us," and shine your flashlight on it.* Jesus also said that he, the light, came to save people. Jesus told Nicodemus that we don't have to walk around in the darkness that comes from not knowing God. Let's move on. *Lead children to the last sheet.* This sheet reads, "People who believe in Jesus live forever with him in heaven." This is the best, most wonderful thing Jesus told Nicodemus. Just as this flashlight leads us around the room, Jesus leads us to God. *Open your Bible to John 3:16, and shine the flashlight on the page so children can see it.* In John 3:16,

Jesus told Nicodemus, **"For God so loved the world that he gave his one and only Son, that whoever believes in him shall not perish but have eternal life."** If we believe in Jesus, we get to live forever with him in heaven! *Shine the flashlight on a cross or similar symbol in the room.*

Let's look at the light and thank God for sending Jesus, the light of the world. Dear God, thank you for sending Jesus, the light of the world, to lead us to you. We love you. In Jesus' name, amen.

Since Jesus is the light of the world, let's shout, "Jesus is the light" three times and see what happens. Ready? Go! *Lead children in shouting three times, and have a volunteer turn on the lights after the third shout.*

Jesus Notices a Widow's Giving

Bible Story: Mark 12:41-44

> **Bible Verse:** "Each man should give what he has decided in his heart to give, not reluctantly or under compulsion, for God loves a cheerful giver" (2 Corinthians 9:7).

Simple Supplies: *You'll need a Bible, and two pieces of chewing gum for each child.*

I'm so glad you're here today. Let's begin in an unusual way. I'm going to give each of you a piece of gum. Please hold on to it without chewing it. *Distribute the gum.* Now I'd like you to think about the gum you're holding. What do you think the gum tastes like? *Pause for children to respond.* Now I'd like you to think about something really silly. Let's imagine that every person needs one piece of gum each day to live and that you're holding your last piece of gum. Now imagine that your best friend asks you for your piece of gum. What would you do? *Pause.* It might be hard to give up your gum, huh?

The Bible tells a true story about a very poor woman who was in a similar situation. She had almost no money. One day in church, she gave her last bit of money to God. Jesus noticed what she'd done. He told his disciples that even though the woman gave only a very little bit of money, it was as if she'd given more than anyone because she gave to God something she really needed. That would be like giving up your last piece of gum.

God loves it when we—like the woman in the Bible story—are happy to give to him. *Open your Bible to 2 Corinthians 9:7, and show the page to the children.* Second Corinthians 9:7 says, **"Each man should give what he has decided in his heart to give, not reluctantly or under compulsion, for God loves a cheerful giver."** This verse tells us we aren't to give because someone *makes* us; instead, we're to give because we *want* to, because we're happy to. It's not always easy to give away things we love or need, but God can help us. Let's pray and ask him to help us. Dear God, we know you want us to give happily, so please help us to do just that. Thank you for giving us things that we can give away. In Jesus' name, amen.

Now that you know what the Bible says about giving, I'd like you to try it. If you want to, you can give your piece of gum to someone in the congregation. You don't have to, but you can if you want to. *Give kids a minute to give away their gum. Then call them back.* You did a great job of giving away your gum! If you liked giving away your gum, please stand, hold your hands over your head, and clap. If you really miss your gum, please sit and clap. Ready? Go! *Pause.* Now if you received a piece of gum and really appreciate it, I'd like you to clap. *Lead the congregation in clapping.* Do you see how it makes other people feel when we give things to them? That's exactly how God feels when we give things to him.

Thank you for helping me today. You've been great! Please take a piece of gum as you go. *Distribute one piece of gum to each child.*

People Rejoice as Jesus Enters Jerusalem

Bible Story: Mark 11:1-11

Bible Verses: "At the name of Jesus every knee should bow, in heaven and on earth and under the earth, and every tongue confess that Jesus Christ is Lord, to the glory of God the Father" (Philippians 2:10-11).

Simple Supplies: *You'll need a Bible, palm branches, and a volunteer to play the part of Jesus. Before the sermon, explain the volunteer's role to him or her. You may even want your volunteer to wear a robe as a costume.*

'd like all the children to meet me at the back of the room today. *Walk to the back of the room to meet the children.* Hello, everyone. Today we're going to talk about an important day in Jesus' life. He was entering the city of Jerusalem, and the people were so excited that he was coming to their city. What are some things that excite you? *Pause for children to respond.* Does anyone know why the people were excited that Jesus was coming to Jerusalem? *Pause.* The people thought Jesus was going to be their king. As he rode into Jerusalem, they put palm branches and their coats on the road. *Distribute the*

palm branches. As Jesus rode into the city, the people shouted, "Hosanna! Hosanna in the highest!" That's similar to when we shout "Hooray!" Some people walked in front of Jesus, and some walked behind him. They shouted "Hosanna!" and waved palm branches in the air. It was a wonderful day!

I have a surprise visitor for you today; we'll pretend he's Jesus. Let's form two lines. *Help kids form two lines.* As "Jesus" enters, wave your palm branches and shout "Hosanna!" as loudly as you can. Some of you may even want to lay your palm branches down for Jesus to walk on, just as the people of Jerusalem did. *Have your volunteer "Jesus" enter the room. Encourage the children to follow Jesus and to keep shouting. You may want to have your volunteer walk around the room to give the children more time to escort Jesus to Jerusalem. Have the volunteer lead the children to the front of the room.*

That was fun! *Open your Bible to Philippians 2:10-11, and show the page to the children.* Philippians 2:10-11 says, **"At the name of Jesus every knee should bow, in heaven and on earth and under the earth, and every tongue confess that Jesus Christ is Lord, to the glory of God the Father."** We can praise Jesus and confess, or say, that Jesus is our Lord. Just as the people in Jerusalem praised Jesus with palm branches, let's praise Jesus by doing the following: I'll read this Scripture again. When I say the name "Jesus," everyone kneel. When I've finished reading the verse, shout, "Jesus Christ is Lord!" Let's practice that line first. "Jesus Christ is Lord!" *Read Philippians 2:10-11 again, kneeling on the word "Jesus" and then shouting. Have kids repeat the sentence a few times, shouting louder each time.*

It's exciting to praise Jesus! Let's stay on our knees as we pray. Dear God, we praise you and confess that Jesus Christ is our Lord. Thank you for sending Jesus to us. Amen.

Jesus Rises from the Dead

Bible Story: Mark 16:1-8

> Bible Verse: "Jesus said to her, 'I am the resurrection and the life. He who believes in me will live, even though he dies' " (John 11:25).

Simple Supplies: *You'll need a Bible, an empty cookie box, and a full box of cookies.*

As the children come forward, pretend to eat cookies from the empty cookie box. Hello, everyone. These sure are good cookies. Would any of you like one? *Pass around the empty box.* How come you aren't getting any cookies? *Pause for children to respond.* The box is empty? Well, how can that be? It was full of cookies a minute ago. I guess I ate the whole box of cookies.

How did it make you feel to think you were getting some cookies and then to find out there was nothing there? *Pause.* The same thing happened in the Bible to some women. Jesus had been killed, and the women were very sad. They went to where Jesus was buried to visit his grave. But do you know what? A big stone that had been used to close Jesus' grave had been moved! Do you think we could lift this [item]? *Name something heavy in the room, such as a pew or podium.* Well, the stone that was used to seal Jesus' grave was much bigger and heavier than the [item]. Can you imagine the women's surprise when they saw that the stone had been moved? Tell me about a time you were very, very surprised. *Choose a few children to share.* Then you know how surprised the women were.

They looked to see if Jesus' body was there, and they got another surprise. A man in a white robe was sitting there. He told the women that Jesus had risen from the dead! How do you think this news made the women feel? *Pause.* They might have felt a little like you did when you tried to get a cookie out of an empty box.

Open your Bible to John 11:25, and show the page to the children. John 11:25 says, **"Jesus said to her, 'I am the resurrection and the life. He who believes in me will live, even though he dies.' "** Jesus died for us because he loves us and wants us to someday live in heaven with him. When you believe in Jesus, he's always with you. *Hold up the empty box of cookies.* Instead of living an empty life, like this empty cookie box, with Jesus we can have a full life, like this full box of cookies. *Hold up the full box of cookies.*

Let's pray and thank God for raising Jesus from the dead, and then I will share these cookies with you. Dear God, thank you for sending Jesus to save us by dying on the cross and coming to life again. In Jesus' name, amen. *Distribute the cookies.* As you fill your stomach with a cookie, think of how you can ask God to fill your heart and life.

Jesus Appears to His Disciples

Bible Story: John 20:19-31

> Bible Verse: "Now faith is being sure of what we hope for and certain of what we do not see" (Hebrews 11:1).

Simple Supplies: *You'll need a Bible and a bean seed.*

Hold up a bean seed. Can anyone tell me what this is? *Pause for children to respond.* That's right! It's a bean seed. What will happen if I put this seed in dirt, water it, and put it in the sun? *Pause.* How do you know this bean seed will grow? *Pause.* We don't know for certain that it will grow, but because it's a normal bean seed like other bean seeds that grow, we can have faith that it will grow.

Just as we can have faith that the seed will grow, we can have faith in Jesus. After all, he came to earth as a baby, grew up, died, and rose from death. After he rose, he appeared to many people so they would know he really was alive. Even so, one of Jesus' followers named Thomas didn't believe that Jesus had risen. Thomas said he wouldn't believe Jesus had risen until he saw him and touched him. It was as if Thomas couldn't believe that bean seeds grow into plants. So Jesus appeared to Thomas to show Thomas he really was alive.

Who can tell me what the word "evidence" means? Evidence is what proves something is true. We use evidence to build our faith. For example, let's look at the evidence that proves this is a bean seed. *Hold up the bean seed, and encourage children to look at it and touch it. Don't let young children hold it because it's a choking hazard for them.* How do you know this is a bean? *Pause.* That's right! It's shaped like a bean and looks like a bean. Do you have faith that this is a bean? *Pause.* Because of the evidence, you know it's a bean.

We can also use evidence to build our faith in Jesus. *Open your Bible to Hebrews 11:1, and show the page to the children.* Hebrews 11:1 says, **"Now faith is being sure of what we hope for and certain of what we do not see."** So faith means we can believe in something even if we don't see it. Because we have evidence of Jesus in the Bible and in our lives, we can believe in him even though we don't see him.

Let's talk to God about this. Dear God, thank you for giving us evidence of Jesus in the Bible and in our lives. Help us to have faith in Jesus. Thank you. In Jesus' name, amen. When you get to your seat, draw a picture of a bean to remind you that you can believe in Jesus.

Jesus Sends Power from God

Bible Story: Acts 2:1-21; 3:12-19

> **Bible Verse:** "But the Counselor, the Holy Spirit, whom the Father will send in my name, will teach you all things and will remind you of everything I have said to you" (John 14:26).

Simple Supplies: *You'll need a Bible and a soft pompom for each child. These are available in craft stores in bags of assorted colors and sizes.*

I'd like to start by giving you each a pompom. *Distribute pompoms to the children.* What do you like about the pompoms? *Pause for children to respond, and compare each response to the Holy Spirit.* Pompoms are soft, which is comforting. The Holy Spirit is like that by making us feel comfortable and loved. Pompoms are colorful. The Holy Spirit is like that by adding color to our lives. When we do what the Spirit asks us to do, we find goodness and happiness. *Add comparisons based on children's responses.*

One of the neatest things about the Holy Spirit is the way the Spirit came to Jesus' followers after Jesus went back to heaven. People from many different countries had come to a city called Jerusalem to celebrate a holiday. Jesus' followers were there too. Suddenly a sound like a big wind filled the house where Jesus' followers were staying. Then Jesus' followers saw what looked like flames of fire on each of them. Let's put our pompoms on our heads to help us imagine what that must have been like. *Put a pompom on your head.* What do you think Jesus' disciples thought about the wind and flames of fire? *Pause.*

The people who had come to Jerusalem heard the sound like a big wind, and they found Jesus' followers. Remember that these people were from many different countries, and they spoke different languages. But the Holy Spirit helped Jesus' followers speak the languages of everyone there because it was so important for people to hear about Jesus.

Jesus had told his followers about the Holy Spirit. *Open your Bible to John 14:26, and show the page to the children.* As you hear what Jesus said, listen for how the Holy Spirit helps us. John 14:26 says, **"But the Counselor, the Holy Spirit, whom the Father will send in my name, will teach you all things and will remind you of everything I have said to you."** How does the Holy Spirit help us? When you have an answer, hold up your pompom. *Choose a few children to share.* You listened so well! The Holy Spirit teaches us about God and reminds us of what Jesus taught.

Let's thank God for sending the Holy Spirit. As we pray, shake your pompoms to tell God "thank you." Dear God, thank you for sending your Holy Spirit so we can know you better and remember what Jesus taught. Amen.

You may have a hard time understanding the Holy Spirit. That's OK. Christians everywhere sometimes have trouble understanding the Holy Spirit. But God will help you just as he helped Jesus' followers—by sending the Holy Spirit. Take your pompoms with you as a reminder that God's Holy Spirit is with you.

Peter Tells the Sanhedrin About Jesus

Bible Story: Acts 4:5-14

> **Bible Verse: "Have I not commanded you? Be strong and courageous. Do not be terrified; do not be discouraged, for the Lord your God will be with you wherever you go" (Joshua 1:9).**

Simple Supplies: *You'll need a Bible, one-half sheet of colored construction paper for each child, and tape.*

How many of you have ever been afraid? *Pause for children to respond.* What kinds of things make you afraid? *Choose a few children to share.* The Bible tells a true story about two men named

Peter and John. They had to meet with some angry men, and they could have been very afraid. What do you do when you're afraid? *Pause.* Peter and John weren't afraid because they had someone to help them and tell them what to say to the angry men. Who helps you when you're afraid? *Pause.* Peter and John had a special friend who helped them be strong and gave them courage. Their friend was the Holy Spirit sent by God.

Did you know that the same Holy Spirit wants to help you when you're afraid, too? *Open your Bible to Joshua 1:9, and show the page to the children.* Joshua 1:9 says, **"Have I not commanded you? Be strong and courageous. Do not be terrified; do not be discouraged, for the Lord your God will be with you wherever you go."** God sends the Holy Spirit to help us wherever we are and whenever we're afraid.

Let's make something to remind us of how the Holy Spirit will help us. *Distribute the construction paper to children. Show children how to roll their papers into megaphones, then tape the papers in place. Be sure to make a megaphone for yourself.* Hold up your paper to your ear like this. *Demonstrate how to hold a megaphone to your ear as an earphone.* I'll whisper words from the Bible in your ear to help you the next time you're afraid. *Whisper in each child's ear, "Be strong and courageous."* Just as I whispered words in your ear to help you be brave, God's Holy Spirit will whisper words and thoughts to you when you're afraid.

Do you think we should share the words I whispered to you with the congregation? *Pause.* When I count to three, let's hold our papers up to our mouths and shout the words from the Bible. *Show children how to hold their papers like megaphones. You may need to remind them of the words "Be strong and courageous." On the count of three, lead kids in shouting the words to the congregation.*

That was great! Let's thank God for the Holy Spirit. Dear God, thank you so much for sending your Holy Spirit to us to help us when we're afraid. Help us to listen to your Spirit. In Jesus' name, amen. Don't forget to take your megaphones home to remind you that the Holy Spirit will help you when you're afraid just as he helped Peter and John.

Philip Tells the Ethiopian About Jesus

Bible Story: Acts 8:26-40

> **Bible Verses:** "But the fruit of the Spirit is love, joy, peace, patience, kindness, goodness, faithfulness, gentleness and self-control" (Galatians 5:22-23).

Simple Supplies: *You'll need a Bible, a piece of paper for each child, and one for yourself.*

I'm trying to fold this paper into an airplane. Can someone tell me how to do this? *Allow several children to give advice.* Thank you all for helping me. How did you know how to fold paper airplanes? *Pause for children to respond.* How do you know how to do other things? *Pause.* You learn how to do things when others teach you and when you practice. When you need help with something, it's a good idea to ask someone who knows how to do it. I'm glad I asked you.

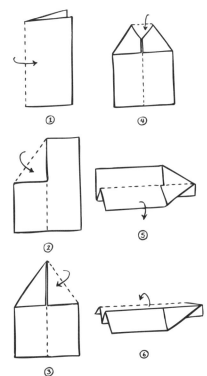

We need that kind of help, too, as Christians. We need people to teach us who Jesus is and help us live as Christians. In the Bible, a man named Philip helped another man learn about Jesus. While I tell you about Philip, you'll fold an airplane using the steps I learned from you to show how we teach each other. It will help you remember to learn from each other. I'll tell you when to fold. *Distribute the sheets of paper. You may want to demonstrate how to make the folds by folding your paper again as you read the following story.*

An important man was traveling in a foreign land. Make the first fold in your airplane. As he traveled, he read the Bible.

Make the folds to form the nose of the plane. The man was reading a passage in the Old Testament, but he couldn't understand the passage. Make the next fold of your plane. Philip heard the man reading, ran up to him, and asked, "Do you understand what you are reading?" Make the next fold of your plane. The man didn't understand, so Philip began with the passage the man was reading and told him all about Jesus. Make the fifth fold. As the two traveled and talked, they came to some water. The man asked Philip to baptize him. Make your final fold. Now fly your planes to celebrate that the man learned about Jesus and believed in him. *Pause.*

To fly your plane, you must use your arm as a tool. God gives Christians, like the man in the story, tools that help them live for God. These tools are called the fruits of the Holy Spirit. These tools help us live as Christians. *Open your Bible to Galatians 5:22-23, and show the page to the children.* Galatians 5:22-23 says, **"But the fruit of the Spirit is love, joy, peace, patience, kindness, goodness, faithfulness, gentleness and self-control."** Let's talk about how each of these fruits of the Spirit help us live as Christians. How can patience help us live as Christians? *List each fruit of the Spirit, and pause for children to respond.*

Let's thank God for these tools, these fruits that help us live as Christians. Dear God, thank you for teaching us to live as Christians, just as Philip taught the man in our Bible story. Help us to live as Christians by living with love, joy, peace, patience, kindness, goodness, faithfulness, gentleness, and self-control. In Jesus' name, amen.

Peter Visits Cornelius

Bible Story: Acts 10:1-44

> **Bible Verses:** "Therefore go and make disciples of all nations, baptizing them in the name of the Father and of the Son and of the Holy Spirit, and teaching them to obey everything I have commanded you. And surely I am with you always, to the very end of the age" (Matthew 28:19-20).

Simple Supplies: *You'll need a Bible, enough inflated red balloons for half the children, enough green balloons for half the children, and a* *large trash bag. Before the sermon, hide the inflated balloons in the trash bag.*

Have children form two groups, and have the groups sit down at least five feet apart. *Say the following in an "important" voice.* I'm so glad you're here today because I have some important advice for you. I have different advice for each group. Please be patient as I give the other team advice. *Stand with your back to one group but facing the other group, and whisper the following:* Here's my advice: When you see red and green things, bat them into the air. *Walk to the other group, stand with your back to the first group, and whisper the following:* Here's my advice: When you see red and green things, toss them into the air. *Turn to both groups to say the following:* Please don't share the essential advice I've given you with the other group. Do you know why I've given you this advice? *Pause for children to respond.* Well, it'll be clear in a minute. Now I want you to shut your eyes. *Distribute the balloons to the second group.* OK, open your eyes and follow my advice. *Help batters hit the balloons and tossers toss the balloons at the batters. After a minute, collect the balloons.*

Great job following my advice! Did my advice help you know what to do? *Pause.* This reminds me of a true story in the Bible. God told Peter to tell a man named Cornelius about Jesus. God also told Cornelius to find Peter. Just as I gave the groups different advice, God gave Peter and Cornelius different advice. My advice helped you play a game, but God's advice to Peter and Cornelius helped everyone in Cornelius' house to believe in Jesus.

God wants us to do exactly what Peter did. He wants us to tell others about Jesus. A passage in the Bible tells us exactly what to do. *Open your Bible to Matthew 28:19-20, and show the page to the children.* Matthew 28:19-20 says, **"Therefore go and make disciples of all nations, baptizing them in the name of the Father and of the Son and of the Holy Spirit, and teaching them to obey everything I have commanded you. And surely I am with you always, to the very end of the age."** A disciple is a follower of Jesus, and Jesus wants us to make disciples. How do you think we're supposed to make disciples? *Pause. Be sure to affirm their answers to this difficult question.* Jesus says we're to make disciples all over the world, and we can start by making disciples right where we live. What are some things we can do in our own town to make disciples? *Allow children to answer, and affirm their responses.* Jesus wants us to tell others about him just as Peter told Cornelius about Jesus. It's important to remember that Jesus said he'd always, always be with us. He can help you tell others about him.

 Let's ask Jesus for help in telling others about him. Dear God, we want to tell others about you, but it's hard sometimes. Please help us tell others about you. Thank you for always being with us. In Jesus' name, amen.

Take a balloon with you to help you remember to tell others about Jesus. *Distribute balloons to the children.*

SECTION

FOUR

SUMMER
QUARTER

God Tests Abraham

Bible Story: Genesis 22:1-18

Bible Verses: "So be careful to do what the Lord your God has commanded you; do not turn aside to the right or to the left. Walk in all the way that the Lord your God has commanded you, so that you may live and prosper and prolong your days in the land that you will possess" (Deuteronomy 5:32-33).

Simple Supplies: *You'll need a Bible, a straw for each child, and a cup of water for each child.*

Who can tell me some reasons you give for not doing what you're told? *Choose a few children to share.* Sometimes it's easier to make an excuse than to do what we're asked. But something happens when we don't do what we're asked. *Give each child a straw.*

Bend your straw, then try to straighten it out. The bend stays. Now this straw will be difficult to drink from. Just as you put a bend in your straw, when you make excuses instead of doing what God tells you, you put bends in your life. It's then difficult to straighten out your life. God promises that if you do what he tells you, your life will be better. *Open your Bible to Deuteronomy 5:32-33, and show the page to the children.* Deuteronomy 5:32-33 says, **"So be careful**

to do what the Lord your God has commanded you; do not turn aside to the right or to the left. Walk in all the way that the Lord your God has commanded you, so that you may live and prosper and prolong your days in the land that you will possess." When we do what God tells us to, our lives are better. Sometimes God asks us to do difficult things, but we feel great when we do those things well.

Distribute cups of water to the kids. Use your straw to drink your water. You'll have to work to straighten out the bends in your straw. While you work, I'll tell you a true story from the Bible.

God promised a man named Abraham that he would have a son. Abraham had to wait years and years, but finally his son was born. Then God asked Abraham to do something very hard. God asked Abraham to give up his son. What's it like to have to give up something you really love? *Pause.* It's very hard. Of course, Abraham didn't want to give up his son, but he did what God asked. When Abraham obeyed, God was pleased. God even gave Abraham's son back to him. What's it like to get something you really love? *Pause.* Well, then you can imagine how happy Abraham was that he'd obeyed God, pleased God, and gotten his son back.

God wants us to obey as Abraham did. Even when God asks you to do really difficult things, he wants you to obey. Can you think of some things God wants you to do? *Pause.* What great ideas! God asks us to do some fun and easy things, and God asks us to do some hard things. But God promises that if we obey him, our lives will be better. Let's ask God to help us obey. Dear God, help us to obey you even when you ask us to do hard things. Thank you for promising us better lives. In Jesus' name, amen.

Isaac Marries Rebekah

Bible Story: Genesis 24:1–66

> **Bible Verse:** "If any of you lacks wisdom, he should ask God, who gives generously to all without finding fault, and it will be given to him" (James 1:5).

Simple Supplies: *You'll need a Bible, a small plastic container that seals well, a small plastic jar of vinegar, baking soda, and a trash bag. Before the sermon, hide all the items except the baking soda, which you should keep hidden and close to you. Hide the other ingredients where children will easily find them.*

How would you like to see a neat science experiment? I've got a great one to show you today. Oh, wait a minute! I can't find any of my supplies here. I must have dropped them as I walked in. Could you help me look around for a small plastic container, a small jar of vinegar, and a trash bag? *Help children look for the ingredients.* Thanks for your help.

This reminds me of a Bible story. One of Abraham's servants was looking for a woman to marry Abraham's son Isaac. Just as you searched for these ingredients, Abraham's servant traveled a long way and searched all over for the right wife. The servant needed help just as I needed help.

OK, now for the science experiment. *Hold up the small plastic container, and speak in a mysterious voice.* This special container is very important. You're going to be amazed because I can create mysterious foaming stuff right before your eyes. *Open the container, and show kids the inside.* What do you see? That's right—nothing. *Place the open container on the trash bag.* Next we need special foaming liquid. *Pour about one-half cup of vinegar into the container.* Now for the amazing part. Watch and be amazed! *Place the lid on the container, shake it, drop it on the plastic, and back away. Wait a few seconds.* We've got a problem. *Approach the container slowly, open it carefully, and look inside.* It's not working. *Shake the container, drop it, and back away.* Why isn't this working? Can you help me remember what I've done? *Pause for children to respond.*

Thank you! Now I remember that I'm missing a special ingredient. This is kind of like Abraham's servant again. The last we heard about him, he was looking for a woman to marry Isaac, and he needed help. He needed a special ingredient. Do you know what he did? He prayed and asked God for wisdom. Who can tell me what wisdom is? *Pause.* That's right! And guess what. Just after the servant prayed for wisdom, God showed him who Isaac should marry. Awesome, huh? The special ingredient for our science experiment is kind of like wisdom: It helps things happen the way they're supposed to.

Oh, I remember where I left the special ingredient. *Retrieve the baking soda. Open the container, pour a few tablespoons of baking soda into the container, close the container, shake it gently, and then remove the lid. Allow kids to watch the vinegar and baking soda foam for a few moments. Then seal the container, and set aside the ingredients.*

We needed a special ingredient for our experiment to work, and Abraham's servant needed wisdom to find a wife for Isaac. We, too, sometimes need to stop and ask God for wisdom, that special ingredient. *Open your Bible to James 1:5, and show the page to the children.* James 1:5 says, **"If any of you lacks wisdom, he should ask God, who gives generously to all without finding fault, and it will be given to him."** If we ask God for wisdom, he'll give it to us.

With what things in your life do you need wisdom from God? Maybe you don't know how to help a friend, or maybe you need help in obeying your parents. *Pause.* Let's pray and ask God to give us wisdom. You can silently tell God what you need help with. Dear God, you've told us that if we ask for wisdom, you'll give it to us. We need your wisdom about these things. *Pause.* Thank you for giving us wisdom. In Jesus' name, amen.

Let's finish with a cheer. We'll shout "wisdom" three times. Ready? One, two, three. Wisdom! Wisdom! Wisdom!

Jacob Deceives Esau and Isaac

Bible Story: Genesis 25:27-34; 27:1-40

> **Bible Verse:** "The Lord detests lying lips, but he delights in men who are truthful" (Proverbs 12:22).

Simple Supplies: *You'll need a Bible and a gift-wrapped box.*

pen your Bible to Proverbs 12:22, and show the page to the children. Proverbs 12:22 says, **"The Lord detests lying lips, but he delights in men who are truthful."** What does it mean to lie? *Pause for children to respond.* When we lie, we don't tell the truth. Our Bible verse says God doesn't like us to lie but wants us to tell the truth. Let's learn what lying did to a family in the Bible. That can help us understand why God wants us to tell the truth all the time.

I'd like you to act out this story, so I'll need you to form two groups. I want all the children who are older brothers and sisters in one group, and I want all the children who are younger brothers and sisters in the other group. If you're a middle brother or sister, or if you have no brothers or sisters, you may choose which group you'd like to be in. *Help children form two groups, and have the groups stand and face each other.* As you listen to the story, I'll show you when and how to act out your part. Members of the older group are the older son in this story. His name was Esau. *Have the "Esau" group members bow.* Members of the younger group are the younger son. His name was Jacob. *Have the "Jacob" group members bow.*

Who can tell me about a very special gift you've received? *Choose a few children to share.* Those are special gifts. Because Esau was older, his dad promised to give him a very special gift someday. *Hold up the gift-wrapped box.* The gift would give Esau a good future and a good life, so it was very, very special. *Place the gift-wrapped box between the two groups, but closer to the Esau group.* If you were Esau, how would you feel about getting that special gift? *Pause.* If you were Jacob, how would you feel about not getting that special gift? *Pause.*

Now Esau liked to hunt, so I'd like the Esau group to pretend to shoot a bow and arrow. *Demonstrate pretending to shoot a bow and arrow.* Jacob liked to stay at home, and he was at home one day cooking stew. I'd like the Jacob group to pretend to stir a stew. *Demonstrate pretending to stir a stew.* While Esau was hunting, he became very hungry. *Lead the Esau group in rubbing their stomachs.* Then he became even hungrier. *Lead the Esau group in pointing to their mouths.* When he finally got home, he saw Jacob cooking stew. *Lead the Jacob group in stirring.* Esau begged Jacob for some stew. *Lead the Esau group in clasping their hands and saying "please."* Jacob was smart. *Lead the Jacob group in pointing to their heads.* Jacob told Esau he could have some stew only if Esau promised to give Jacob the very special gift. Esau agreed. *Lead the Jacob group in clapping and cheering, and push the gift-wrapped box closer to the Jacob group.* Think about a very special gift you've been given. Would you give that gift away for some stew? Would you give that gift away for anything? *Pause.* It looks as if Esau didn't care very much about the gift.

Years and years went by, Esau and Jacob grew up, and finally the father, Isaac, said he was ready to give the special gift to Esau. *Lead the Esau group in clapping and cheering, and push the gift-wrapped box closer to the Esau group.* First Isaac asked Esau to go hunting and fix him a special meal, so Esau left. *Lead the Esau group in pretending to shoot a bow and arrow.* The men's mother, Rebekah, told Jacob that Esau was going to get the special gift. *Lead the Jacob group in giving the thumbs-down sign.* Rebekah told Jacob to trick his father into giving him the gift instead. Jacob really wanted that special gift, so he decided he would trick his father. *Lead the Jacob group in rubbing their hands together as if plotting.* Rebekah fixed a special meal, and Jacob dressed up like Esau. He wore Esau's clothes and even put fur on his arms since Esau's arms were hairy. *Lead the Jacob group in rubbing their arms.* Then Jacob took the special meal to his father, Isaac. Isaac had grown very old and his eyesight was failing. Isaac asked Jacob again and again if he was Esau. Each time, Jacob lied. *Lead the Jacob group in nodding.* Jacob told Isaac that he was Esau. And so Isaac accidentally gave Jacob the special gift. *Push the gift-wrapped box to the Jacob group, and lead the Jacob group in cheering.* Just then, Esau came home from hunting. Esau and his father found out that Jacob had lied, but it was too late. *Lead the Esau group in pretending to cry.* Isaac was very sad, and Esau hated his brother. *Have the two groups turn their backs to each other.*

How did Jacob lie? *Pause.* Do you think it was OK for Jacob to lie since Esau had given Jacob the gift for some stew? *Pause for children to respond, then have the two groups face each other and sit down.* Let's remember what our Bible verse says. Proverbs 12:22 says, **"The Lord detests lying lips, but he delights in men who are truthful."** What happened to Jacob and Esau because of Jacob's lie? *Pause.* Why does God want us to tell the truth? *Pause.* Even if we don't think we're being treated fairly, God doesn't like us to lie. What could Jacob have done instead of lying? *Pause.* Those are great ideas! How do you think the story would have ended if Jacob hadn't lied? *Pause.* So what can you do the next time you want to lie? *Pause.* Those are great ideas too.

Let's pray about lying. First I'd like the Jacobs to shake hands with the Esaus. *Pause.* Now keep holding hands as we pray. Dear God, thank you for teaching us not to lie. Lies hurt people just as lies hurt Jacob and Esau. Help us to tell the truth. In Jesus' name, amen.

Jacob Marries Leah and Rachel

Bible Story: Genesis 29:15-30

> **Bible Verse:** "And we know that in all things God works for the good of those who love him, who have been called according to his purpose" (Romans 8:28).

Simple Supplies: *You'll need a Bible, big and colorful stickers, and small and plain stickers.*

Hold up the big and colorful stickers. If you do seven jumping jacks, I'll give you each a sticker. *Pause for kids to do seven jumping jacks.* What would you think if I told you that instead of giving you these big, colorful stickers, I was going to give you these small, plain stickers? *Hold up the small and plain stickers, and pause for kids to respond.* I'm not being very fair, am I? *Distribute the small stickers.* I think everything will work out, though. Wait and see.

This is just what happened in the Bible to a man named Jacob. Jacob wanted to marry a woman named Rachel. Rachel's father said Jacob could marry Rachel if he worked for seven years. Because Jacob loved Rachel, he worked very hard for Rachel's father for seven years. Let's do a jumping jack for each year Jacob worked for Rachel's father. *Lead kids in doing seven jumping jacks.* One, two, three, four, five, six, seven. That's a long time to work! After all those years, Jacob said he was ready to marry Rachel. But Rachel's father tricked Jacob, and Jacob accidentally married Rachel's older sister Leah. What do you think about the trick Rachel's father played on Jacob? *Pause.* What do you think Jacob felt like? *Pause.* What would you have done if you were Jacob? *Pause.*

Open your Bible to Romans 8:28, and show the page to the children. Romans 8:28 says, **"And we know that in all things God works for the good of those who love him, who have been called according to his purpose."** This verse tells us that if we love God, things will work out. How do we act if we love God? *Pause.* How do those actions help things work out for us? *Pause.* Let's see how things worked out for Jacob.

Rachel's father said Jacob could marry Rachel if he worked another seven years. Jacob agreed. Let's do seven more jumping jacks for the seven additional years Jacob worked. *Lead kids in seven jumping jacks.* So Jacob got to marry Rachel after all. *Distribute the colorful stickers to the children.* How did Jacob show by his actions that he loved God? How can we show by our actions that we love God? *Pause.* Those are great ideas! Jacob loved God, and things worked out for him. When we face hard times, we can remember that things will work out for us too. Tell me about some hard times you've faced. *Choose a few children to share.* When you're going through hard times, how can you remember that things will work out? *Pause.* Thank you for those ideas.

Let's pray about those hard times. I'll start and finish the prayer, and you can talk to God about your hard times. Dear God, we now want to tell you about our hard times. *Pause.* Help us to remember that because we love you, things will work out. Thank you for helping us through these hard times. In Jesus' name, amen. As you return to your seats, find two friends and tell them, "Things will work out for those who love God."

Joseph Dreams Disturbing Dreams

Bible Story: Genesis 37:1–11

Bible Verse: "A new command I give you: Love one another. As I have loved you, so you must love one another" (John 13:34).

Simple Supplies: *You'll need a Bible, baby wipes, a trash can, small cookies, and Band-Aid bandages.*

The Bible tells a true story about a boy named Joseph who had strange dreams. Let's act as if we're asleep and having dreams. *Encourage children to lie down and snore as if they're sleeping.* Joseph dreamed that he and his brothers each had gathered a bundle of grain. In his dream, Joseph's bundle of grain stood tall. Let's all stand tall like Joseph's bundles of grain. *Lead children in standing tall.* In Joseph's dream, his brothers' bundles of grain bowed down to his bundle of grain. Let's all kneel. *Lead children in kneeling.* In another dream, the sun, moon, and eleven stars bowed down to Joseph. Now Joseph had eleven brothers, so it was interesting that eleven stars bowed down to Joseph.

If you had a brother with these kinds of dreams, what would you think about them? *Pause for children to respond.* Well, when Joseph told his family about his dreams, his brothers became angry and jealous. What does it mean to be jealous? *Pause.* Let's make a face like Joseph's brothers might have made. *Lead children in making angry faces.* Was it right for Joseph's brothers to be angry? *Pause.* Joseph's brothers should have loved him instead of being jealous. *Open your Bible to John 13:34, and show the page to the children.* John 13:34 says, **"A new command I give you: Love one another. As I have loved you, so you must love one another."** God wants us to love one another, so let's practice being loving.

Have kids form pairs. Decide which partner will be leader 1 and which will be leader 2. I'm going to call out either "leader 1" or "leader 2" and then instructions for that leader. Leader 1, say, "You're dirty" to your partner, and wash his or her hands. *Distribute the baby wipes. Have kids throw away the used wipes.* It's very loving of you to help your friend get clean. Leader 2, say, "You need love," and tell your partner some-thing you like about him or her. *Pause for kids to respond, and help the younger children.* It's very loving of you to say nice things to your friend. Leader 1, say, "You look hungry," and feed your partner a cookie. *Distribute the cookies.* It's very loving of you to feed your friend. Leader 2, say, "You're hurt," and put a bandage on your partner's hand. *Distribute the bandages, and help children who need it.* It's very loving of you to help your friend.

You did a great job in being loving! What are some other ways you can show love to others? *Pause.* We can love others by helping them, encouraging them, doing things with them, and so on. There are lots of ways we can love others. Let's thank God for the chance to love people. Dear God, thank you for giving us the chance to love people as you do. Please help us love others. In Jesus' name, amen.

Be sure the children have each eaten a cookie before returning to their seats.

Joseph's Brothers Sell Him Into Slavery

Bible Story: Genesis 37:12-36

> **Bible Verse:** "Do not follow the crowd in doing wrong" (Exodus 23:2a).

Simple Supplies: *You'll need a Bible, a marker, and two pieces of paper. Write "cheer" in large letters on one piece of paper, and write "boo" on the other piece.*

Hi, everyone. This morning, we're going to start our time together with a game. Let's play Simon Says. I'll give you some instructions, but you should follow my instructions only if I say, "Simon says" first. *When children understand how to play, give them several instructions such as "Simon says, 'Stand up,'" "Simon says, 'Pat your head,'" and so on. Be sure to sprinkle in some instructions without saying "Simon says" first—"Turn around" or "Touch the ground," for example.*

Have children who follow those instructions sit down. Finish with the fol-lowing: Simon says, "Rob a bank." *Pause for children to respond.* Wait a minute. We aren't supposed to rob banks, are we? *Pause.* God has something to say about following others in doing something wrong. *Open your Bible to Exodus 23:2a, and show the page to the children.* Exodus 23:2a says, **"Do not follow the crowd in doing wrong."** What do you think that means? *Pause.* Right! We shouldn't do wrong things even when other people do.

I'm going to tell you a true story from the Bible about some brothers. When you hear that a brother does something good, put both your hands in the air and cheer. When you hear that a brother does something wrong, put both your thumbs down and boo. Let's practice. Joseph hugged his brother. *Hold up the "cheer" sign, and lead children in cheering with their hands in the air.* Great! Now try this one: Judah hit Joseph. *Hold up the "boo" sign, and lead children in booing with their thumbs down.* Good!

OK, here's the story. Don't forget to cheer and boo. There was a boy named Joseph who had many brothers. He loved his brothers very much *(cheer),* but his brothers were very jealous of him *(boo).* One day Joseph's brothers became so jealous they decided to kill Joseph *(boo).* One brother, Reuben, loved Joseph and talked the other brothers out of killing Joseph *(cheer);* but Reuben talked his brothers into capturing Joseph and putting him into a deep well *(boo).* Reuben planned to rescue Joseph later *(cheer).* So the brothers captured Joseph *(boo).* Later, some men came by, and Joseph's brothers sold him to the men as a slave *(boo).* The men took Joseph far away, and his brothers told their father that Joseph had been killed *(boo).* You all did a wonderful job cheering and booing!

Joseph had eleven brothers, so it must have been hard for one brother to disagree with all the others. But let's remember what our Bible verse said. Exodus 23:2a says, **"Do not follow the crowd in doing wrong."** How did Joseph's brothers, including Reuben, follow the crowd in doing wrong? *Pause.* When do you feel like doing what everyone else is doing? *Pause.* Sometimes it's hard to do what's right when everyone else is doing wrong. But God tells us not to do wrong even if everyone else does.

Let's play Simon Says again. *Play Simon Says again, and end with the following:* Simon says, "Break a window." *Watch for kids' response.* You've learned not to follow the crowd in doing wrong! Let's not forget that God asks us to do what's right, no matter what our friends, brothers, or sisters do.

Let's pray. Dear God, thank you for teaching us to do what is right. Help us to not follow the crowd in doing wrong. Help us to always do what's right. In Jesus' name, amen.

Pharaoh Puts Joseph in Charge

Bible Story: Genesis 39:20–41:49

Bible Verse: "Humble yourselves, therefore, under God's mighty hand, that he may lift you up in due time" (1 Peter 5:6).

Simple Supplies: *You'll need a Bible, corks, a large bowl of water, and hand towels. Choose corks (available in hardware stores) that are large enough not to be choking hazards.*

Have kids gather around the bowl, and give each child a cork. Corks are so light that they float in water. No matter how many times I push down the cork, it bobs back up to the top. *Push your cork into the water, and watch it bob to the surface.* Now you can take turns trying to push your corks under the water. *Give each child a turn to push a cork into the water.*

Now we'll use our corks to learn a Bible story. *Through-out the story, lead kids in pushing their corks down and letting their corks bob up. If you have more than five children, have them take turns.* A man named Joseph may have felt like this cork sometimes. He did the right things, but he kept having hard times. *Push the cork into the water.* Even in bad times, Joseph kept doing the right things. *Let the cork bob up.*

Once someone said Joseph did something wrong, but Joseph hadn't done anything wrong. Have you ever been punished for something you didn't do? *Pause for children to respond.* It's hard to get into trouble for something you didn't do. That's just what happened to Joseph, and he had to go to jail. *Push the cork into the water.* The Bible tells us how to deal with hard times like that. *Open your Bible to 1 Peter 5:6, and show the page to the children.* First Peter 5:6 says, **"Humble yourselves, therefore, under God's mighty hand, that he may lift you up in due time."** Instead of trying to force others to see how great we are, we should wait for God to make it happen.

That's just what Joseph did. While he was in jail, the warden, or the man in charge of the jail, saw how smart Joseph was. The warden put Joseph in charge of all the other prisoners. *Let the cork bob to the surface.* Joseph didn't become hateful because he was sent to jail. He knew God would lift him up. Even though Joseph did a good job, the warden kept him in jail. *Push the cork down.*

Once the Pharaoh, or the king, put two of his workers in jail. Both of these workers had dreams. God helped Joseph know what the dreams meant, and he helped the two workers. *Let the cork bob up.* When one of the workers left the jail, Joseph asked the worker to help him get out of jail. The worker promised, but then he forgot. So Joseph had to stay in jail. *Push the cork down.*

Two whole years passed. Then Pharaoh, the king, had strange dreams that no one could understand. Then the worker remembered Joseph, and Pharaoh brought Joseph out of jail. *Let the cork bob up.* God helped Joseph know what the dreams meant, so Joseph helped Pharaoh. Pharaoh was so happy that he asked Joseph to be second in command, under only Pharaoh! So Joseph went from being in jail to being the second most powerful man in the country! Just as our Bible verse teaches, Joseph humbled himself and waited for God to lift him up.

Why is it sometimes hard to be humble? *As children share, have them push their corks down.* How can we remember to be humble and wait for God to lift us up? *As children share, have them let their corks bob up.*

Let's pray. Dear God, help us know how to be humble. Help us lean on you when hard times push us down. Thank you for helping us to bob up like corks. In Jesus' name, amen.

Take your corks with you as a reminder to be humble and to bounce back, confident that God will help you.

Joseph Forgives His Brothers

Bible Story: Genesis 42:1–45:28

> **Bible Verse:** "Bear with each other and forgive whatever grievances you may have against one another. Forgive as the Lord forgave you" (Colossians 3:13).

Simple Supplies: *You'll need a Bible, small cups, and jelly beans. Before the sermon, place five jelly beans in a cup for each child.*

Today, let's talk about forgiveness. Can someone tell me what it means to forgive a person? *Pause for children to respond.* Good! Forgiving someone means you've stopped being mad or sad at that person for hurting you. We're going to practice forgiveness today, just as Joseph in the Bible did. *Open your Bible to Genesis 42:1–45:28, and show the passage to the children. Then hand a cup of five jelly beans to each child.* While I'm telling the story about Joseph, I want you all to wander around the room as if you're Joseph's brothers traveling from Canaan to Egypt. When I say that Joseph cried, you should find a partner and tell each other about a time you may have hurt someone. Then you'll give each other one jelly bean and say, "I forgive you as the Lord forgave me." Then you'll eat the jelly bean your partner gave you. Are you ready? Remember to listen for when Joseph cries.

When Joseph was a boy, his brothers had sold him into slavery. Joseph had been taken to Egypt—a long, long way from home—where he grew up to be the second most powerful man in the country. But Joseph's brothers didn't know what had happened to him. Many years later, Joseph's brothers needed food. They had to go to Egypt to buy food. Joseph was in charge of the food, and he recognized his brothers. But his brothers didn't recognize him, and he pretended to be a stranger. Joseph told his brothers to go home and bring back their youngest brother, and the brothers were afraid. They thought they were being punished. When Joseph heard this, he realized his brothers were sorry. He began to cry. *Have kids share with their partners and exchange and eat the jelly beans.*

Hold your partner's hand. Dear God, thank you for the friends who forgive us. Thank you for giving us forgiving hearts. Amen. Let's continue.

Remember to listen for when Joseph cries.

Joseph had slipped silver coins into his brothers' bags, and the brothers thought it was a test to see if they would keep the money. So they returned to Egypt with gifts of spices and nuts, and double the amount of silver! They also brought their youngest brother with them. When Joseph saw this brother, he began to cry. *Have kids find new partners and exchange and eat their jelly beans.*

Hold your partner's hand while we pray. Dear God, it's not always easy to admit when we've done something wrong. Please help us to tell others when we're sorry. Amen. Let's continue.

When the brothers left to go home with more food, Joseph had a silver cup hidden in the youngest brother's bag. Joseph wanted to see how his brothers would treat their youngest brother. He wanted to know if they had changed and if they were sorry for what they'd done to him all those years ago. When Joseph said he was going to make the youngest brother his slave for taking the cup, the other brothers begged Joseph not to take him. Joseph was touched by how much his brothers cared, and he began to cry. *Have kids again find new partners and exchange and eat their jelly beans.*

Again, hold your partner's hand while we pray. Dear God, it's not easy to forgive someone who does something wrong to us. Please help us to keep love in our hearts. Amen.

Let's finish the story. Joseph finally told his brothers who he was. He told his brothers not to be afraid or angry with themselves for hurting him so many years ago. When his brothers realized Joseph was telling the truth, they were so happy! They hugged each other, and Joseph cried with joy! *Have kids again find new partners and exchange their jelly beans.*

It can be hard to forgive. It was hard for Joseph, but he knew that God wants us to forgive. *Open your Bible to Colossians 3:13, and show the page to the children.* Colossians 3:13 says, **"Bear with each other and forgive whatever grievances you may have against one another. Forgive as the Lord forgave you."** God forgives us when we ask and wants us to forgive others just as he does. God knows we're happier when we forgive others.

Close your eyes, and eat your last jelly bean while we pray. Dear God, thank you for forgiving us and for helping us forgive others. Help us to remember how much you love us so we can share that love with others. In Jesus' name, amen.

God Protects Moses

Bible Story: Exodus 1:1—2:10

Bible Verse: "God is our refuge and strength, an ever-present help in trouble" (Psalm 46:1).

Simple Supplies: *You'll need a Bible, candy, and plastic sandwich bags. Before the sermon, put a piece of candy into a bag for each child. Then hide the bags in the sermon area.*

Hello, everyone. Today we're going to talk about a group of people called the Israelites. They lived in the land of Egypt, and they were slaves to a very mean Pharaoh, or king. Can someone tell us what a slave is? *Pause for children to respond.* Pharaoh was so mean that he made the Israelites do very hard work. Let's pretend you are the Israelites and I am the very mean king. *Have the children stand.* I'll tell you what to do, and you pretend you're doing it. While you act, talk about how hard the work is. For example, you could say, "This work is making me so tired" or "I just can't keep up with all this work." Ready?

Give children instructions such as "Dig a hole," "Build a wall," "Plant seeds," and so on. Be sure to give directions relevant to the time period. As children work, say things such as "That's just not good enough. You'll have to work harder." After a minute, have children sit down again.

How did it make you feel to do all that hard work? How did you feel when the Pharaoh said those things to you? *Pause.* Well, you know just how the Israelite people felt. But even though they were suffering, God was with them. They had lots of babies, and they were strong and healthy. But this also made the Pharaoh mad. He told the midwives, who were like nurses who helped the women have their babies, to kill all the baby boys who were born. What a mean, mean Pharaoh! But the midwives knew it was wrong to kill, so they didn't do it. Have you ever decided not to do something wrong even if someone else wanted you to do it? *Pause.* You're very brave, just as the midwives were.

To tell the next part of the story, I've brought a surprise today. It's hidden, so everybody must look for it. *Have kids look for the candy, and give clues if they have difficulty. Be sure each child gets a bag, then call kids back together.*

Sometimes it's fun to look for hidden things, but what if the hidden treasure was a baby? That's what happened in our story. Pharaoh said all the baby boys should be killed, but Moses' mother loved her baby boy and didn't want him to be killed. She hid him in her house for as long as she could. Then, when he got too big to hide in the house, she hid him in a basket and placed the basket in the weeds and bushes in the river. She wanted to protect him from danger. What are some things you would do to protect someone you loved from danger? *Pause.*

This story has a happy ending. The king's daughter found baby Moses, and she asked Moses' own mother to take care of him until he was a young boy. Then Moses lived as the princess' son. God took care of Moses.

Open your Bible to Psalm 46:1, and show the page to the children. Psalm 46:1 says, **"God is our refuge and strength, an ever-present help in trouble."** In hard times, God is strong for us and helps us. God protected the Israelites from the mean king. God helped the midwives do what was right. God protected Moses as he floated in the river. God will also help you. Let's pray. Dear God, thank you for helping us. Help us remember to look to you for help. In Jesus' name, amen.

Moses Meets God at the Burning Bush

Bible Story: Exodus 2:11–3:20

> Bible Verse: "'For I know the plans I have for you,' declares the Lord, 'plans to prosper you and not to harm you, plans to give you hope and a future'" (Jeremiah 29:11).

Simple Supplies: *You'll need a Bible.*

Think of one thing you're good at—one thing you might be chosen to be a leader for—and strike a pose to show us that thing. For example, if you're good at soccer, you could pretend to kick a ball, or if you're really friendly, you could smile and pretend to shake hands. *Pause for kids to pose. You might need to help younger children think of something they're good at, such as hugging or helping others.* Now tell us what you're good at and why you could be a leader. *Choose a few children to share.*

You're all so talented! If you had to choose a leader, what kind of person would you choose? Why? *Pause for children to respond.* Let's think more about choices. What kind of person do you choose to be your friend? Why? What other choices will you have to make in life? What do you think you might choose to be when you grow up? *Allow kids to share.*

I'm going to tell you a true story from the Bible, and I need a volunteer to be Moses and a volunteer to be Pharaoh. The rest of you will be Hebrews. *Choose two volunteers. Encourage "Moses" to stand with his hands on his hips, looking like a leader. Encourage "Pharaoh" to stand with his arms crossed and a mean look on his face. Encourage the "Hebrews" to kneel as slaves before Pharaoh.*

Did you know that God chooses people to do things too? God chose Moses to be a great leader. The Hebrew people were slaves in Egypt, and God wanted someone to ask Pharaoh, the Egyptian king, to let the people go. Moses was the perfect guy for the job because even though he was Hebrew, he grew up in Pharaoh's house and went to an Egyptian school.

But when God told Moses the plan, Moses argued with God. *Ask Moses to pose as if he's arguing with God.* Do you ever argue when your parents ask you to do things? *Pause.* Moses probably sounded a lot like you. He made up excuses and said he didn't think he was good enough. What are some things people ask you to do that you don't want to do? Why don't you want to do those things? Are some of those things good things that you should do? *Pause for responses.*

Leading the people away from Egypt could have been a scary job. On his own, Moses probably wouldn't have been able to do it. But God promised to go with Moses and help him. God knew how things would turn out.

Open your Bible to Jeremiah 29:11, and show the page to the children. Jeremiah 29:11 says, " **'For I know the plans I have for you,' declares the Lord, 'plans to prosper you and not to harm you, plans to give you hope and a future.'"** Just as he chose Moses, God has chosen you to do special things. God has plans for you, good plans. Maybe God will send you to be one of the first people living on the moon, or maybe he will make you a strong leader like Moses. If you follow and obey God even when he asks you to do things you don't want to do, you will live in God's good plans.

Ask kids to return to their original poses. God has given each of you talents that will help you serve God. Stay in your poses, and let's pray.

Dear God, thank you for making each of us special and for making great plans for our lives. Help us to always follow and obey you. In Jesus' name, amen.

The Israelites Receive cruel Treatment

Bible Story: Exodus 5:1—6:1

> **Bible Verse: "But those who hope in the Lord will renew their strength. They will soar on wings like eagles; they will run and not grow weary, they will walk and not be faint" (Isaiah 40:31).**

Simple Supplies: *You'll need a Bible, one length of string for each child, and one Life Savers Gummies candy for each child.*

Have you ever had a job to do that was almost impossible? *Pause for children to respond.* Wow! Those sound like difficult jobs. I have a simple and fun job to start us off today. I'm going to give each of you a piece of candy and a piece of string. I'd like you to make a necklace out of these supplies. *Distribute string and candies, and help children make necklaces. Make one for yourself, too.* Great job! Let me ask you something. Do you really like your necklaces? *Pause.* I'm glad you like them. I like mine too. How difficult was it to make these necklaces? *Pause.* I didn't think it was that difficult. I've got another job for you. *Gather children to one side.* I'd like you to move from this end to the other end of this area without using any of your muscles. You can't stand. You can't walk. You can't walk like a crab. Now, one at a time, I'd like you to get to the other side. But remember, you can't move a muscle. Ready? Go! *If children try to walk, crawl, or move any limb to get to the other side, remind them that it's not allowed. Children will begin to understand that this is an impossible task.* Why aren't you getting to the other side? *Pause.*

You know, something similar happened to a group of people called the Israelites. A king, Pharaoh, gave Israelites jobs to do. They weren't fun jobs like making necklaces out of string and candy; they were impossible jobs like trying to cross a big area without using their muscles. The Israelites were treated very poorly, but they kept trusting that God would help them. *Open your Bible to Isaiah 40:31, and show the page to the children.* Isaiah 40:31 says, **"But those who hope in the Lord will renew their strength. They will soar on wings like eagles; they will run and not grow weary, they will walk and not be faint."** People who trust that God will help them have hope and strength from God. That's a wonderful promise, isn't it?

When we feel as if we've got something impossible to do, God wants us to trust him. God wants to help us do things that feel impossible. Let's pray about trusting God to help us. Dear God, thank you for promising that when we trust you, you will help us. Help us to be patient and wait for you to give us strength. In Jesus' name, amen.

Now let's try that impossible task again. *Gather children at one end of the area.* When I say "go," fly like an eagle to the other side. Ready? On your mark, get set, go! *Allow children to run from one side to the other. Then have them "soar" back to their seats.*

God Sends Plagues on Egypt

Bible Story: Exodus 7:8–12:30

> **Bible Verse: "Great is our Lord and mighty in power; his understanding has no limit" (Psalm 147:5).**

Simple Supplies: *You'll need a Bible.*

Today we're going to talk about power. Where do we get power? What kinds of power are there? *Prompt kids to mention power sources such as electricity, gasoline, wind, sun, and muscle power.* It's difficult to imagine what our lives would be like without these power sources. Now think about a special kind of power that's more powerful than any other kind of power: God's power.

The Bible tells us a lot about God's power. When a group of people called the Israelites were treated very poorly by a Pharaoh, or king, God's power helped them break free from the Pharaoh. Just as the

Israelites felt powerless against Pharaoh, we sometimes feel powerless. Let's play a game to see what that feels like. While you play, we'll learn more about God's power. *Have kids play a game of Power Tag. Have them form groups of four and link elbows. Designate one group to be "It" and another group to be the "Power Player." Groups may only take baby steps, heel to toe. "It" and the Power Player may take regular steps. Once "It" tags a group, that group has to freeze in place. If the Power Player tags a frozen group, that group may move again. Tell kids that periodically throughout the game, you'll call out "Freeze!" and all groups will freeze where they are. As kids play, remind them to walk instead of running. Have kids start play.* Freeze! Pharaoh refused to let the Israelites go. God showed power by sending lots of frogs and icky bugs to "bug" the Pharaoh! Let's pretend we have itchy bug bites all over our bodies. *Have kids "scratch" for a moment and then return to the game.* Freeze! Pharaoh still wouldn't let the people go. God gave the Pharaoh's people yucky sores all over their bodies to show power. Let's say "Ouch!" and rub our arms to pretend we have sores on our bodies. *Let kids return to the game.* Freeze! Pharaoh still wouldn't let God's people go. So God showed power by sending lots of hail to rain down. Let's cover our heads and pretend we're in a hailstorm. *Let kids return to the game.* Freeze! Pharaoh still wouldn't let God's people go, so God covered the land with darkness. Let's pretend we can't see anything because it's too dark. God showed power because he wanted Pharaoh to let the Israelites go. Let's sit down now.

How did it feel to be chased by someone who could move a lot faster than you could? Tell me about a time you felt like that in real life. *Choose a few children to share.* How is God like the Power Player in the game? *Pause.* I'd like to share a Bible verse with you about God's amazing power. *Open your Bible to Psalm 147:5, and show the page to the children.* Psalm 147:5 says, **"Great is our Lord and mighty in power; his understanding has no limit."** God loves us so much, and God's power helps us just as it helped the Israelites in the Bible story.

Let's make big arm muscles and thank God for his power. *Lead kids in making muscles.* Dear God, thank you for loving us and helping us, especially when we feel powerless. In Jesus' name, amen.

The Israelites Escape From Egypt

Bible Story: Exodus 12:31-42

> **Bible Verse:** "So if the Son sets you free, you will be free indeed" (John 8:36).

Simple Supplies: *You'll need a Bible, clear tape, and yellow crepe paper.*

After all the children have come forward, hang the yellow crepe paper around the group and instruct children not to cross it. Have any of you ever heard the phrase "all tied up"? What do you think it means? *Pause for children to respond.* Well today we're going to discover what it would be like to be tied up and unable to do normal things. For a long time, a group of people called the Israelites were tied up and unable to do the things they wanted. I wonder what that might have been like. Let's see.

First find a partner. *Have kids form pairs.* Now turn your back to your partner, stand touching back to back, and don't break away from your partner. Now reach down, and straighten your socks or tie your shoes. *Pause.* Great job! How difficult was that? *Pause.* We're just getting started! The Bible says the Israelites were tied for a long time.

Let's make things a little more difficult. Face your partner and join hands. Don't ever let go. Follow me and walk around with your partner. *Attempt to lead pairs outside the circle. When you get to the crepe paper, pretend you can't cross it. Go another direction, and do the same thing.* Wow, this is strange. We can only go so far, and then we have to stop. What do you think we should do to get through? *Pause.* Well let me tell you what God did for the Israelites. God sent a man named Moses to talk with the Pharaoh, who was keeping the Israelites tied. Let's try that. When I count to three, yell, "Hey, hey! Let us go!" *Count to three, then lead kids in yelling. Then try to break through the barrier, but fail.*

Next God showed power to the Pharaoh. Let's try that. Let's flex our arm muscles and yell, "Hey, hey, let us go!" *Lead children in flexing and yelling. Try to break through the barrier again, but fail.* Finally Moses and God showed the Pharaoh that they meant business. Let's try that. Let's shake our fingers and say, "Hey! We mean business!" *Lead the children in this. Break through the crepe paper, then lead kids in walking around the area as you cheer and clap. Lead kids back to the sermon area.* Wow! It worked! The Israelites were freed just as we were!

This reminds me of a Bible verse. *Open your Bible to John 8:36, and show the page to the children.* John 8:36 says, **"So if the Son sets you free, you will be free indeed."** Just as God set the Israelites free, God wants to set us free. God will set us free from doing wrong things if we ask. Let's ask God to do that right now.

Dear God, you've promised us that if we ask, you'll set us free. Please forgive our sins and set us free from doing wrong things. In Jesus' name, amen. *Have kids march back to their seats, waving their hands as a symbol of being set free.*

Scripture Index